Defense Against the Dark

Defense Against the Dark

A FIELD GUIDE TO PROTECTING YOURSELF
FROM PREDATORY SPIRITS, ENERGY
VAMPIRES, AND MALEVOLENT MAGICK

Emily Carlin

Illustrations by Daniele Serra

New Page Books
A Division of The Career Press, Inc.
Pompton Plains, N.J.

DEFENSE AGAINST THE DARK
EDITED AND TYPESET BY KARA KUMPEL
Cover design by Ian Shimkoviak/The Bookdesigners
Illustrations © Daniele Serra.

Printed in the U.S.A.

To order this title, please call toll-free 1-800-CAREER-1 (NJ and Canada: 201-848-0310) to order using VISA or MasterCard, or for further information on books from Career Press.

The Career Press, Inc.
220 West Parkway, Unit 12
Pompton Plains, NJ 07444
www.careerpress.com
www.newpagebooks.com

Library of Congress Cataloging-in-Publication Data

Carlin, Emily.

    Defense against the dark : a field guide to protecting yourself from predatory spirits, energy vampires, and malevolent

    magic / by Emily Carlin.

    p. cm.

    Includes bibliographical references (p.) and index.

    ISBN 978-1-60163-170-1 -- ISBN 978-1-60163-656-0 (ebook) 1. Protection magic. I. Title.

BF1623.P75C37 2011

130--dc22

2010054605

This book is dedicated to all of the wonderful witches and wizards who have helped me along this journey.

ACKNOWLEDGMENTS

Special thanks go to The Grey School of Wizardry for inspiring this project and helping me make it happen.

Heartfelt thanks go to my parents. Your support and understanding has never wavered no matter how far down the rabbit hole I've gone. I don't say it often enough, but you mean the world to me.

Many thanks go to my wonderful husband, Ty, who is endlessly patient and supportive of my weirdness.

To my wonderful friends who not only put up with my weirdness but love me for it. Susie, Kristen, and Alix—I adore you. Rae—your support for this project from its inception has been breathtaking and I can never thank you enough for keeping me excited, even when I felt overwhelmed.

Massive thanks go to all my friends and colleagues at the Grey School. Without you, this project would have remained an idea floating in the back of my brain to all eternity. Special thanks go to Moonwriter for showing me that writing a book was actually possible and to Rainmaker for continually inspiring me to excellence.

Contents

Part II
Magickal Protection

Introduction

DEFENSE AGAINST THE DARK

There are more things in heaven and in earth, Horatio,
than are dreamt of in your philosophy.
—William Shakespeare, *Hamlet*

Just because you're paranoid doesn't mean an invisible
demon isn't about to eat your face.
—Jim Butcher

When we lie awake, listening to the sounds of the night, we imagine all the things that could be making those strange noises. We know, of course, that the rumble is the sound of the refrigerator coils, the knocking is from the old furnace, and the creaking is nothing more than the house settling...isn't it? For all that we try to convince ourselves, somewhere in the back of our minds we ask, *What if that wasn't the refrigerator? Did I just hear a voice?* For 99 times out of a hundred it was just the refrigerator, but what about that one time it was something else? For all that the modern world has beaten back the world of the unseen, taught us that it couldn't possibly exist, we know that things exist for which science has yet to account. Our ancestors knew it, and took precautions to protect themselves from what they couldn't understand rather than hiding under the covers and hoping the impossible would go away.

A skeptic might ask what proof there is for the existence of an unseen magickal world. The only answer is this: Seeing is believing. At some point in their lives, most people experience something they simply cannot explain—lights moving in the garden that couldn't be flashlights, voices shouting in an empty house, objects moving of their own accord. We laugh and slough off these experiences, attributing them to sleep deprivation or bad sushi. But if we looked at them more closely instead of ignoring them, we might see something more.

This book does not require you to believe. All I ask is that you approach this subject with an open mind. The symptoms caused by the presence of unseen entities or magick can be felt by anyone. Many of us have had moments when we've seen movement out of the corners of our eyes or felt a sense of intense foreboding in an empty room. These are

Introduction

some of the most common indications that there is more going on than meets the eye. The methods I suggest for dealing with particular sets of symptoms are things that folklore, magickal wisdom, or experience have shown to alleviate the symptoms. If you find yourself tripping on nothing and keep finding your keys in the oddest places (and you don't have children), you can perform a simple banishing. If the phenomena stop, does that mean you had pixies or goblins in your home? Probably! But does it really matter? If the symptoms exist and the suggested methods alleviate them, what more is needed? Don't shun ritual or folkloric remedies just because they seem silly; you've little to lose by trying, and a lot to gain.

The world of the unseen is full of wondrous things: Faeries and sprites dance in the moonlight when they think we're not looking, and most of the powers and beings that dwell outside our normal perceptions are benign, or at least have no interest in us. Unfortunately, not all metaphysical creatures are good. Just as there are good and bad people in this world, so are there good and bad denizens of the unseen. Many of the creatures who dwell outside of the mundane see the world from a completely different perspective. What may seem wrong from our point of view might be perfectly reasonable or even virtuous from theirs. They may not mean us specific harm, but may do it nonetheless. Most of what people encounter of the unseen world is simply annoying, the result of curious or bored creatures playing and testing boundaries.

Other creatures are less ambiguous. There are creatures dwelling in the darkness who delight in frightening or harming human beings. The world of popular fiction is rich with fantastic tales of malignant creatures from the depths of the abyss who seek to destroy our world. This makes for truly compelling reading, but it doesn't teach us much about what's actually out there. Fiction is just that: fiction. Truly malevolent beings are incredibly rare. Malevolent beings with vast and horrific magickal powers are rarer still. If they existed with anything like the profusion found in fiction, the world would have been overrun long ago. Yes, there is an infinitesimally small chance that you might come across such a creature, but don't bet on it. Be cautious with the unseen. Protect yourself. But don't worry too much.

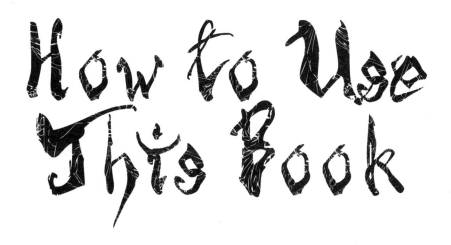

How to Use This Book

At its heart, this book is a guide to magickal defense against all the things that go bump in the night. This is not an introductory text on defensive magick. Part II, Methods of Removal, does include information on the basic mechanics of magickal self-defense, but it is by no means exhaustive on the subject. This book will give you enough information to deal with any negative magickal encounter you are likely to have. It will teach you how to protect yourself and deal with the immediate effects of negative magick and malicious creatures, and instruct you on when you should seek the help of a more experienced magickal practitioner. If you ever feel that a magickal situation puts you or others into real physical danger, please seek help immediately. Better to have help and not need it than to really need help when it's nowhere to be found.

Further, this book does not assume that you already practice magick, but it does assume that you are open-minded when it comes to metaphysics. I feel fairly safe in that assumption because you wouldn't have bothered with this book if you thought it was nonsense. Though anyone can benefit from the information in this book, it will be most helpful to people who have some basic knowledge of magick and how the metaphysical world works. In certain entries you will find explanations for what people with metaphysical sensitivity can expect to feel in the presence of certain entities. If you are not metaphysically sensitive, don't worry. Just ignore that information and move on. If you would like to learn how to train yourself to be more metaphysically sensitive, I highly recommend *Grimiore for the Apprentice Wizard* by Oberon Zell-Ravenheart. If you find yourself interested learning more about the basics of magick and magickal practice, I recommend training at the Grey School of Wizardry (*www.greyschool.com*).

This guide will attempt to give you some basic information on the less pleasant denizens of the unseen world so that if you happen to encounter them, you'll know what to do. It would be impossible to write an exhaustive guide to all the things you might possibly encounter, so I won't try. This guide is confined to the types of malignant magick and creatures of the night you might actually come across, such as ghosts and pixies, and a few things whose myths are so prevalent that it would be a crime to exclude them, such as vampires and revenants. What you will not find here are detailed entries on creatures who are nothing more than a physical menace. This is a magickal guide and will only spend time on creatures against which magickal defenses are useful.

For each entry in this guide, you will find information on how common a creature is, how dangerous it is, how difficult it is to get rid of, as well as a short explanation of *what* the creature is, the most common lore surrounding it, and exactly how to get rid of it. The vital statistics also include common symptoms that you can use to identify what kind of phenomenon you're actually dealing with. Be advised that many different phenomena share the same or similar symptoms. You will have to read through the descriptions to determine the likeliest explanation for the symptoms you've experienced. For removal, many entries will direct you to a specific method described either in the entry itself or at the back of the book.

Some entries describe not a single creature, but several similar creatures. For example, there is a single entry on Merfolk that covers several different kinds of fish-people from different areas of the world.

How to Use This Book

They are grouped under a single entry because, although they may be different creatures, the information that a person would need to know upon encountering any one of them is the same. The creatures have roughly the same apparent symptoms and methods of removal. Although the folklore surrounding these creatures may be wildly different, it wouldn't make much of a difference to someone who actually came across one. If you find that you desire more information on any particular creature, a quick Google search is likely to lead you to as much folklore as you could ever want.

A Quick Note on Terminology

In this guide you will often see the terms *practitioner* and *magickal practitioner*. I use these terms to mean anyone who consciously practices magick in any way. I prefer these terms to the more common *witch*, *wizard*, *sorcerer*, or *warlock* because these terms are burdened by connotations. Any of them can be used simply to denote someone who practices magick, or can be used specifically to mean someone who practices baneful or malignant magick. At one time or another, all of these terms have been used derogatorily, but in recent years, various members of the magickal community have reclaimed them, using them as proud badges to show they are unashamed of who they are and what they do. Unfortunately, that means we are left with no simple term to denote someone who practices magick malignantly. Perhaps this is a good thing, as people and their motives are always complicated. Perhaps no one should be branded as a bad practitioner.

You will also notice that I spell *magick* with a "k." This is a convention in parts of the magickal community to separate real magick from stage magic. Real magick is meant to effect some kind of change in the world, whereas stage magic is sleight-of-hand or illusion. Of course, magic and magick can be combined to great effect, but that is another topic entirely.

KEY TO VITAL STATISTICS

For each entry in this guide, you will find the following vital statistics rated on a scale of 1 to 10:

- Danger Level
- Rarity
- Difficulty of Removal

For **Danger Level**, the scale is as follows:

1: No intrinsic danger.

2–3: May appear frightening, and will likely be annoying, but not harmful.

4–5: Will likely be troublesome and may do tricks, but is unlikely to cause real harm.

6–7: Can be quite frightening and can cause mild physical harm under extreme circumstances.

8: Has been known to cause serious mental or physical harm.

9: Can be deadly.

10: Can be deadly to many people.

For **Rarity**, the scale is as follows:

1: Extremely common; you've probably seen it several times, but didn't know it.

2–3: Most people will encounter this once or twice in their lives.

4–5: Some people will experience this; perhaps 1 in 10.

6–7: Few people will experience this; perhaps 1 in 1,000.

8–9: Very rare; will be experienced perhaps once in a generation.

10: Unheard of. No record of this actually being experienced.

How to Use This Book

For **Difficulty of Removal**, the scale is as follows:

1–2: Anyone can remove it quickly and easily.

3–4: May require a basic cleansing or banishing ritual.

5–7: May require a strong cleansing or banishing ritual.

8–9: Will require a strong cleansing or banishing done by an experienced practitioner.

10:   Requires expert attention and possibly divine intervention.

Part 1

A Field Guide to Magickal Creatures and Occult Happenings

- 1 -

Faeries

GENERAL PROTECTION

Folklore tells us several methods that can protect one from many different kinds of Fay. Possibly the most common protection against faeries of all types is to carry a piece of iron, such as a nail, charm, or horseshoe. It is believed that most faeries are repelled by iron and that it can even be harmful to the touch. Conventional wisdom also holds that most faeries are repelled by salt, holey stones (small stones with *natural* holes in them, most often found on rocky beaches or near waterfalls), St. John's Wort, the sound of bells, and twigs of the broom plant. Some lore also tells that faeries cannot cross running water; however, this would not hold true for water faeries.

Though different faeries have many different characteristics, folklore agrees that all faeries are extremely proud. If one should encounter a faery of any type, it should be treated with respect and never be made light of. For this reason, people often speak of faeries as "The Good

Folk" or "The Fair Folk" when one might be within earshot because some believe that the Fay find the terms *faery* and *fairy* disrespectful. Such consideration costs people very little and could make life much, much easier. For more extensive information on faery etiquette, I recommend *A Witch's Guide to Faery Folk* by Edain McCoy.

Some lore also say that faeries that have targeted a particular person for their wrath can be outwitted by simple trickery. If one has been targeted by a faery, one can simply turn one's clothes, most often a jacket or sweater, inside out. This superficially changes a person's appearance and is believed to confuse the faery into thinking its target is someone else. Similarly, some lore holds that pointing one's shoes away from the bed can make Faeries that would do mischief overnight believe that their target has gone in the direction the shoes point. Such lore is common and may be effective against very simple Fay, but it should not be relied upon alone when dealing with the more clever and dangerous faeries.

Bean-sidhe

VITAL STATISTICS

Danger Level: 1-2
Rarity: 8
Difficulty of Removal: N/A
Where Found: Within hearing distance of an old Irish family.
Common Symptoms: A frightening keening or screaming heard immediately preceding a death in the family.

LORE

The Bean-sidhe is also known as the Banshee, Bean-nighe, or Bean-chaointe. This frightening but largely harmless faery is seen by members of certain families, usually of Irish descent, immediately preceding a death in the family. It is believed that a Bean-sidhe will attach itself to a family and remain with it for many generations, following the family wherever it goes. Though originally from Ireland, the Bean-sidhe is now found wherever Irish émigrés have settled, particularly in the American southeast.

In older folklore, the Bean-sidhe only attach themselves to the great families of Ireland; in modern times this may have changed. As the Irish emigrated into the wider world, many of their faeries, including the Bean-sidhe, followed. And, just as the Irish have settled into their new homes and integrated into new cultures, so have the Bean-sidhe. Though they are still far more common among Irish families, it is believed that some Bean-sidhe have attached themselves to non-Irish families that have caught their notice. Lack of Irish descent is no longer a guarantee against encountering a Bean-sidhe.

Bean-sidhes always appear as females, usually old and haggard in appearance. Their bodies may appear to be fully corporeal, indistinguishable from a human woman, or they may appear translucent and wraith-like. They are most often described as wearing gray cloaks, a winding sheet, or torn grave clothes, though they are sometimes seen wearing simple peasant garb. Most often appearing standing or floating near the home of the soon-to-be-deceased, the Bean-sidhe is often only noticed when she begins her characteristic keening or wailing. Sometimes they are seen only as a face at the window, or are not seen at all—only heard. The keening of the Bean-sidhe has been described as anything from violent shrieks, thin weeping, or even almost musical ululations.

Sometimes Bean-sidhes give their death omen in a slightly different guise. In some stories, a Bean-sidhe will appear as a hunched woman washing bloody clothes in a stream. In such situations, they usually do not keen, but instead look sadly at the relative of the soon-to-be-deceased. In these cases, she is usually called a *Bean-nighe*. The most famous story of such an omen comes, unsurprisingly, from Irish folklore. It is said that before his last fatal battle, the great champion Cú Chulainn sees an old woman washing bloody armor identical to his in a river. The woman looks sadly at him and he realizes that the coming battle will be his last.

There are differing opinions on the origins of Bean-sidhes. In some lore, they are spirits of human women who died in childbirth. Sometimes they are doomed forever, and sometimes only doomed to fulfill their office until the time when they would have died naturally. In other lore, they were never human to begin with.

Methods of Removal

A Bean-sidhe appears for a very limited time, usually only a few minutes. If you tried to make her remove herself, she would likely do so on her own before you'd finished whatever method you'd tried. Consequently, there really isn't anything to do except wait her out.

Never attempt to touch or catch a Bean-sidhe! Although they do not mean us harm when they appear, they are very powerful and have been known to curse those who try to capture them. In the lore such curses are invariably fatal, and often pass on to future generations, as in the famous case of Thomas Reilly: After attempting to catch a Bean-sidhe, Reilly died within a week, his family farm failed, and his descendents suffered from insanity until his line died out. If you leave it alone, a Bean-sidhe will keen for a short while and then leave. Their keening can be frightening, but it's better to have a little scare than lose your life...or worse.

Brownie and Boggart

VITAL STATISTICS

Danger Level: 3-4

Rarity: 6-7

Difficulty of Removal: 5-7

Where Found: Older houses, particularly ancestral homes.

Common Symptoms: For Brownies: small household chores mysteriously finished, kitchen remains clean without much cleaning. For Boggarts: objects thrown, clothes torn without cause, gardens withering despite care.

LORE

Brownies are a benevolent type of household faery. Though originating in Britain, they are believed to have followed emigrants to other lands and are now found all over the world. They are small in stature, usually a little more than 2 feet tall, and have brown, wrinkled skin. Their wrinkled skin gives them the appearance of being very old even when they are quite young.

These faeries are considered household faeries, meaning that they prefer to live in houses with people. They often adopt particular families and move in with them. Some brownies have been known to grow so fond of their human families that they will travel from home to home if their human family moves away. If kept happy, brownies are quite helpful and will assist in doing household chores, such as sweeping, washing dishes, and general tidying. Brownies do not like to be seen by their human family. As result, they almost always do their work at night.

In exchange for helping out around the house, brownies like to receive small gifts of food, such as a bowl of cream or honeyed biscuit left by the fireplace. Brownies can be very particular about how they prefer their homes, and they get angry when their favorite spots (usually the kitchen or fireplaces) are not kept clean. Brownies have been known to show their displeasure by throwing or hiding household items, such as books or dishes.

Also, similar to most faeries, brownies are very proud and will become angry if their human family says negative things about faeries. Never criticize a brownie's work or dismiss them as mere faeries. For this reason, it's tradition to refer to faeries as "The Good Folk" or "The Fair Folk" if you think one might be within earshot. This pride also means that brownies will usually abandon their house if the owners offer to pay them for their work, or if they are offered gifts of clothes. To the brownie, such an offer is an insult, essentially equating them with servants.

If treated very poorly, a brownie can turn into a boggart.

Boggarts are small, mischievous faeries that like to run amok by destroying household goods and harming harvests. Boggarts are very similar in appearance to brownies, but they can always be differentiated by their facial expressions: Brownies retain normal facial expressions, whereas Boggarts always scowl, grimace, or display otherwise nasty expressions.

Boggarts are brownies that have been deeply offended and have gone bad in retaliation. Once a brownie has gone boggart, it will destroy furniture, turn milk sour, rip clothes, ruin harvests—in short, they will do harm to whatever they were helping with before.

METHODS OF REMOVAL

In some lore, a boggart can be placated into turning back into a brownie if the offender corrects the prior offense and leaves generous amounts of cream and honey for it. In other lore, nothing will turn a boggart back into a brownie. In fact, you can't even move away from the boggart, as it will travel around with whatever family it served as a brownie.

The best way of dealing with a boggart is just to be very nice to brownies and hope they don't go boggart in the first place! Brownies are fairly rare these days, and anyone fortunate enough to have one in their household should be careful indeed to keep them happy. So if you wake up one morning and someone has put all your things away (and you know it wasn't someone else in the house), put out a bowl of milk or cream. It's not much to ask.

If you think you've got a boggart, the first thing to do is apologize loudly and clearly to either the boggart itself (if you can see it) or just to the place where you think it is. Then clean the house top to bottom, paying particular attention to hearths and fireplaces. Scrub, mop, sweep, dust, wash the windows, and clean out the closets. Clean everything. Once the house is so clean it shines, leave bowls of cream and dishes of biscuits dripping with honey on each hearth (if you don't have a hearth, leave the dishes on the kitchen counter next to the stove). With any luck, this will placate the boggart and turn it back into a brownie.

Some boggarts are more stubborn than others and can be extremely difficult to remove. If these methods do not work, then you will have to perform a formal banishing ritual. The strong banishing ritual in Part II would be quite effective in removing such a boggart.

Goblin

Faeries

VITAL STATISTICS

Danger Level: 3-7 (The threat posed by the presence of a goblin varies widely and depends on the specific goblin and whether the situation is handled gracefully. If a person panics or seems disrespectful or dismissive, the goblin's behavior is likely to worsen either due to anger or pure enjoyment of causing harm.)

Rarity: 7

Difficulty of Removal: 5-6

Where Found: Residences, forests, caves.

Common Symptoms: Seeing a small, dark mass out of the corner of the eye; household objects being mysteriously broken; seeing a small elf-like creature; spoiled gardens; noticeable lack of wildlife; proliferation of unexplained malignant mischief.

LORE

Goblins are small malevolent faeries, also known as hobgoblins, bogies, or bogles. Goblins are the bullies of the world of Faery—so much so that any small malevolent faery may be called a goblin. In most lore, goblins are of small stature, 2 to 3 feet tall, and look like misshapen elves with characteristic pointed ears. In other lore, goblins appear only as small, dark masses. Their skin is often described as wrinkled and having a green or brown hue. In some lore, they have thin gray hair; in other lore, they are hairless. The stories agree that goblins have grotesque faces with vicious expressions, most often with pointed, needle-like teeth which they take great pleasure in baring to frighten their enemies. In most lore, goblins only move about by night and will seek refuge come dawn, particularly if heralded by the crowing of a cock. It is uncertain if this is because they cannot move about by day or if it is only a preference.

Their behavior can be similar to that of other mischievous faeries such as pixies, but goblins distinguish themselves through the viciousness of their mischief. Less malevolent faeries like to annoy and torment, but their behavior is not malicious—similar to that of a naughty child. Goblins, however, are more malevolent and enjoy causing fear, pain, and destruction. For instance, a pixy might trip someone going down the hallway while carrying books, causing annoyance and maybe a few bruises; a goblin would trip someone walking down a steep flight of stairs, possibly resulting in serious injury or worse. In some lore, goblins are disposed to turn their worst torments towards evil people, such as liars, thieves, and murderers.

Even though they are malevolent, most goblins are not as dangerous as they could be. Goblins are like schoolyard bullies that like to torment because they can. They push, pinch, and frighten, but that is usually the extent of their mischief. They enjoy causing small hurts; it is rarely their intention to cause major mental or physical injury, though they may do so inadvertently. When they do cause more significant harm, it is usually in retaliation for being made fun of or because they believe the person being tormented "deserves it" due to his or her own bad behavior. Of course, woodland and cave-dwelling goblins are another story entirely. More about them in a moment.

Goblins that inhabit residences tend to behave like a very aggressive boggart, so much so that boggarts are sometimes considered goblins. They break household objects, scratch furniture, smash dishes, and spoil food and gardens. They've also been known to trip, pinch, and kick humans, and even to throw objects at them. They can be distinguished from boggarts by the intensity of their actions. Whereas a boggart might spoil your dinner, a goblin would cause it to catch fire and nearly burn down the kitchen.

Woodland and cave goblins are nastier still. Choosing to live deep in uninhabited forests and caves, woodland goblins prefer to have nothing to do with the outside world. They are proud, vicious, and intensely territorial. Woodland goblins have no regard for people, and anyone found trespassing on their territory will face their wrath. Anytime a woodland goblin comes across a human, the goblin will cause the human harm if at all possible. Such goblins often appear in lore as kidnapping and eating children or unwary travelers. Thankfully, they are virtually extinct.

Methods of Removal

It is easier by far to cajole a goblin into behaving than it is to force it from your home. Household goblins can often be appeased into behaving themselves with offers of small gifts, such as cream, biscuits with honey, silver coins, or other shiny objects.

If you cannot convince a goblin to behave, then you must find a way to make it leave. It's always best to begin such efforts by simply asking it to leave, and then commanding it to do so if necessary. If this does not work, then stronger measures will be required. In some stories, it is believed that if you scatter small seeds, such as flax or poppy seeds, on your kitchen floor, the goblin will feel compelled to stop and gather them. This would take so long that the goblin would be unable to complete its task by dawn, and after a few days it would become frustrated and leave the house.

Whereas most faeries abhor cold iron, lore has mixed opinions on whether goblins do. Some lore lists goblins as the only kind of faery that can actually touch or use iron. For this reason, iron is not a recommended goblin repellant. If you feel a strong need for some kind of goblin-repelling object, try a bowl of sea salt or a physical protection charm. Several useful charms are detailed in the Protection Charms and Incantations section in Part II. A strong cleansing ritual should also be sufficient to force it out.

The best way of dealing with woodland goblins is to stay out of their territory. If you find yourself in an oddly blighted wood with an uncanny absence of normal creatures, such as birds or squirrels, there is probably something unpleasant there, and it would be best to leave the area immediately. If you somehow fall into the clutches of woodland goblins, speak to them. Try to mentally confuse them in order to give yourself an opportunity to escape. If you cannot, physical confrontation may be your only recourse—instruction on which is beyond the scope of this guide.

Leanan-sidhe

VITAL STATISTICS

Danger Level: 9
Rarity: 9
Difficulty of Removal: 4-8
Where Found: Near artists and vibrant young people.
Common Symptoms: A beautiful woman makes an offer that is too good to be true.

LORE

The Leanan-sidhe are a very rare type of predatory faery. They appear as mortal women so beautiful that any man would be instantly enthralled. They will appear either attired in the latest and most alluring fashion or in naught but their skin. A Leanan-sidhe will target a young man with a strong life force, often with artistic or athletic talents, and seduce him. She will then lead the young man to a secluded spot and drain his life essence. In this, their behavior is very similar to that of a succubus or other sexual vampire.

There are a few telltale signs that a beautiful woman may actually be a Leanan-sidhe. It is easiest to know if a woman is not what she appears to be when she appears naked out of nowhere! Naked women appearing out of nowhere and attempting seduction are not to be trusted—no woman in her right mind would behave this way. Another way of spotting a Leanan-sidhe is to pay attention to where she comes from. In older lore, the Leanan-sidhe will often emerge from the woods or another uninhabited area. Most beautiful women do not wander the woodlands in their most seductive clothing; any woman doing so would be highly suspect.

In the modern world, a Leanan-sidhe is much more likely to be found in the hottest club in town, and detecting them there is much more difficult.

It's practically impossible to differentiate between a Leanan-sidhe and a woman who is drunk or extremely uninhibited. In such cases, common sense is the best way to safeguard yourself: Stay away from people engaging in highly risky behavior. For those with any kind of psychic ability, the presence of a Leanan-sidhe is likely to make them feel uncomfortable or give them the feeling that something is "off," though they may not be able to identify why. Such feelings can also manifest themselves as stomach aches, headaches, or a prickling sensation at the base of the spine or in the palms of the hands, particularly if the sensitive person touches the Leanan-sidhe. Such feelings do not necessarily indicate the presence of a Leanan-sidhe or any Fay, but they do indicate a strong reason for caution, regardless of the cause.

On certain rare occasions, instead of draining away a man's life force, a Leanan-sidhe will act as a sort of dangerous muse. The faery will offer to grant inspiration and talent to a struggling artist in exchange for a taste of the young man's life force. Such artists subsequently experience a brief period of intense and successful artistic expression. Unfortunately, this creative burst tends to end abruptly and leave the artist burnt out both artistically and physically. Sometimes it will even end in the artist's untimely death.

In some lore, an artist that bargains with a Leanan-sidhe is hers for all eternity. Whereas a man who is simply drained of life by a Leanan-sidhe is free of her at death, a man who bargains with her gives her a hold over his soul that allows her to claim it after his death. Consequently, such a man would be bound to serve her in the realm of the Fay after death.

METHODS OF REMOVAL

Like so many of the Fay, the best way to deal with the Leanan-sidhe is to avoid them. If an ethereally beautiful woman invites you away to a secluded place or offers to give you the gift of artistry, simply take a deep breath and decline. If you don't allow her to lead you away, then she will have no power over you and will do you no harm. In some lore, the man who declines the gift of a Leanan-sidhe's favors gains the kind of power over her that she would have otherwise had over him.

If you or someone you know has managed to fall into the clutches of a Leanan-sidhe, there are a few things that can be done. The most effective thing would be for the person under the faery's power to summon enough willpower to break the enchantment and refuse to cooperate with her, essentially breaking her spell. However, that requires a clear head and tremendous willpower, both of which are unlikely to be present while under an enchantment.

If the will to break the enchantment cannot be summoned, the Leanan-sidhe will respond to most things that typically repel the Fay. Like most faeries, the Leanan-sidhe deplore cold iron. Carrying some iron nails, or better yet an iron horseshoe, will repel her power. They are also said to be repelled by running water. In some lore, calling on the Celtic god Manann, a strong protective entity, will immediately send away a Leanan-sidhe. If none of these things work, a strong hex-breaking ritual may be necessary. (Part II details both regular and strong hex-breaking rituals and how to perform them effectively.)

Merfolk

VITAL STATISTICS
Danger Level: 6
Rarity: 7
Difficulty of Removal: N/A
Where Found: Coastal areas and, more rarely, at sea. Also, in some lakes and rivers.
Common Symptoms: Sailors and fishermen sighting "fish-people."

LORE

Tales of Merfolk abound in every seafaring nation in the world. Some examples include Abere, Ben Varrey, Kelpies, Mambu-Mutu, Merrows, Mermaids, Rusalka, Sirens, and Ukoy. They appear as people, often beautiful women, from the waist up, and fish from the waist down. In many stories (and a lot of artwork), Mermaids are sighted sitting on rocks at the shoreline, combing their hair with one hand and holding a small silver mirror with the other. The glare from the mirror is often what catches the eye of the sailor.

Modern lore, particularly in films such as *Splash* and *The Little Mermaid*, tends to portray Merfolk as kind and humane—basically people with fins. In these modern tales, Merfolk are friendly but shy, often saving people from drowning after sailing mishaps and then disappearing into the depths. Encountering this kind of Merfolk would be an experience of charm and wonder rather than a danger. Unfortunately, there are far fewer accounts of these modern Merfolk than traditional Merfolk.

Unlike the friendly Mermaids depicted in modern lore, most traditional stories of Merfolk depict them as rather vicious. Like the famous Greek Sirens, most Merfolk use their beauty or singing to entrance people into diving into the depths where they find themselves in the Merfolk's power. In most cases, these foolhardy people either find themselves drowned for sport or eaten. The waters where Merfolk live are undoubtedly *their* domain, and any people visiting their waters are mere guests and should treat the Merfolk with respect and a healthy amount of fear.

Tales of Merfolk place them in just about any body of water you can think of. Merfolk seem to be most abundant in the world's oceans and shorelines. The Ben Varrey of the Northern British Isles is an example of ocean-dwelling Merfolk. Ben Varrey look like the sterotypical Mermaid; they have the torso of a beautiful woman with long golden hair and the lower body of a fish. They are believed to swim along ships, particularly fishing vessels, and tempt men into the water by singing and promising their charms. Once the men jump into the water, the Ben Varrey will seize them and wedge them under rocks until they drown; then they feast.

Some Merfolk are found in rivers and even large lakes. The Rusalka of Russia are an example of river- and lake-dwelling Merfolk. The Rusalka is believed to be a half-woman half-fish creature that has the ability to shape-shift into human form and live on land when necessary, though she is very uncomfortable there. Normally Rusalka live in deep lakes and rivers and lure children and young men into the water to drown them. In some stories, Rusalka do so because they are very lonely and want company; unfortunately, they forget that humans have to breathe, and thus their potential playmates do not last long. Traditional Merfolk can be found in any large body of water, so take care.

METHODS OF REMOVAL

If you should catch a glimpse of the Merfolk, simply put it down as a great memory. Do not seek to get closer to them or to find them again the next time you're in the area. If you do, they may try to enchant you or otherwise get you out of your boat and into the water, where you will be at their untender mercy.

If one of the Merfolk tries to entice you into the water, turn your boat away and sail for shore. If it begins to sing, stop up your ears and do not listen. In *The Odyssey*, when sailors were besieged by Sirens, they stopped up their ears and the captain lashed himself to the wheel so he would be physically unable to fling himself into the sea. Modern sound-proofing and headphones should make such extraordinary measures unnecessary. Also, avoid looking Merfolk directly in the eye, as in some stories they are able to hypnotize people with their gaze, and only an act of supreme willpower by their victim can save him or her.

If you find that Merfolk are a continual problem, then you are out of luck. The water is their home and there's nothing, short of thoroughly polluting the water, that will make them leave. The best you can do is bless your boat and hope for the best.

Pixy

VITAL STATISTICS
Danger Level: 2
Rarity: 4
Difficulty of Removal: 2
Where Found: Most common in Britain, but found throughout the world. Dwell in residences, gardens, places of work, and woodlands.
Common Symptoms: Tripping on nothing, having hair pulled, clothing caught on nothing, small shiny objects being "misplaced," getting lost in familiar locations.

LORE

Pixies are a type of very mischievous but non-malevolent faery. These faeries originated in Britain, Cornwall in particular, but have been sighted in numerous other locations. These days pixies can be found indoors and out almost anywhere. They are short, pale, and very thin. They are usually described as having pointed ears and slightly upturned eyes. In some cases, they are also described as having a green or brownish cast to their skin.

During the Victorian era, it was believed that pixies were a race of people condemned to forever remain on earth because they were too bad for heaven and too good for hell. A more recent theory is that pixies were a race of early Picts who inhabited Britain during the Iron Age. Modern archaeologists have found small flint arrowheads on the Isle of Man that they believe were the weapons of the pixy race, but whether they were once a race of humans or not, today, pixies are faeries.

Pixies are famous for their naughty behavior. They are not malevolent; they just do whatever they think is fun and don't think about how that affects others. In this way, their egoism is similar to that of small children—the needs and feeling of others do not figure in their minds. Pixies are known to steal livestock and small, shiny objects, trip people, pull hair, and the like. In modern times, they are most well known for hiding keys and wallets—the ones you swear you just left on that table over there. The behavior they are most famous for in older stories is getting people lost. If you are being "pixy-led," you might find yourself walking down a familiar path when all of a sudden everything looks different and you no longer know where you are. Or perhaps you'll be walking across a field at dusk and find yourself unable to find the gate. In modern times this can translate to that odd loss of concentration that occurs while driving that makes you miss your exit or take a wrong turn.

Pixy behavior is very similar to that of imps, and it can be very difficult to know which entity is responsible for the goings-on. The main difference between the two entities is their motivation: Imps try to hurt and scare people, whereas pixies just try to have fun. For example, if you're carrying a big stack of books and something trips you, then you could be dealing with either a pixy or an imp (or a loose bit of carpet or a cat—

always look for a mundane explanation before looking for a metaphysical one!). If, as you sit on the floor surrounded by the pile of your books, you feel as though you're being laughed at, then you've probably got pixies. If, on the other hand, you feel that something was trying to hurt you, then you probably have an imp. Thankfully, it's not that important to know whether you've got an imp or a pixy because defenses against imps will almost always also work against pixies.

METHODS OF REMOVAL

The classical way to rid yourself of the influence of a pixy is to turn your clothing (usually a jacket) inside out. The theory is that pixy magick is simple and only recognizes a person a certain way, so if you change your appearance (by wearing your jacket inside-out), the magick no longer recognizes you and the spell is broken. Also, as with other faery folk, pixies do not like cold iron. Carrying an iron nail or a horseshoe in your pocket will protect you from almost any kind of faery. However, this will also repel friendly faery folk, so make sure you *really* don't want any faeries around before carrying cold iron.

Another way to deal with pixies is to placate them. Instead of trying to make them go away, simply offer them small shiny objects (like a coin or a thimble), tea, honey, or other sweets in exchange for their promise to behave and not steal things. If you think a pixy has taken something, firmly say "Give [the item] back" or "Please give back my [item]" and then leave the room for a short while, giving the pixies time to return the object. Sometimes you'll find the missing object back where it belongs, or in a place you've already looked for it.

Phooka

VITAL STATISTICS
Danger Level: 4-5
Rarity: 6

Difficulty of Removal: 4
Where Found: Farm country.
Common Symptoms: Nocturnal disturbance of crops and livestock.

LORE

Also known as Puca, Pooka, Kornbocke, Bwca, and Phouka, the phooka are a type of malevolent faery that plagues the countryside, particularly remote farms. Sometimes their presence is similar to that of a rogue wild animal, causing phenomena such as broken fences and a few uprooted crops. Other times they are quite bold, revealing themselves to farmers and demanding tribute. Phooka are only known to move about by night, being frightened by the crowing of cocks and the coming of dawn. Whether they are actually harmed by daylight is unknown.

Phooka are known to be shape-shifters. Their natural form is that of a small, deformed goblin. In this form they can sometimes be physically distinguished from goblins by a pair of large curving horns on their heads and a pair of bright yellow eyes. In some lore, they are thought to have the bodies of goblins and the head of a goat, though they are also known to move about as huge hairy bogeymen, dark horses, and even unnaturally large black eagles. In their natural goblin-like form, they often demand a share of a farmer's crop in exchange for leaving it alone, rather like a gangster extorting protection money from a shopkeeper. Traditionally, the phooka will get anything the farmer failed to harvest before Samhain (October 31). If not given their fair share of the crop, or if harvest is taken after Samhain, phooka are known to destroy crop stores and kill livestock.

Phooka are also known to take the form of a dark horse with bright yellow eyes. In this form, the phooka will ride wildly through the countryside, trampling crops and gardens, frightening livestock, and generally wreaking havoc. In this form, the phooka will also sweep unwary travelers onto his back and give them a wild ride, often for many miles, before throwing the traveler into a ditch or muddy bog. In some lore the phooka will go up to a home and call out the name of the person he wants to take on a ride, causing extensive damage to the property if the person refuses.

Though their behavior can be quite destructive, phooka are not really malevolent. They do destroy property, but they very rarely hurt people. At heart, phooka are nature spirits, and they believe that they are due a measure of deference for "allowing" people to farm in areas that were once wilderness. They believe that asking for a small tithe of the crops from each field is a reasonable request, and indeed, setting aside a few bits and bobs is no great hardship. If they are given respect, then they will do no harm, and can even be benevolent on occasion.

METHODS OF REMOVAL

The easiest way to deal with a phooka is to placate him with gifts. The phooka are known to enjoy freshly picked crops, particularly corn. Leaving such a gift in a basket outside overnight, while specifically stating that it is for the phooka, is likely to keep on from any unwanted mischief. If the phooka is particularly well-pleased by his gifts he may even do a good turn for the farmer or a bit of prophesying for the family (though there are much easier ways of obtaining insight into the future).

However, if you do not wish to placate the phooka, any traditional means of repelling the Fay will work with the phooka. (There is a danger to this, though: If these methods fail to rid you of the phooka, he will become angry and do even worse mischief than before.) Hanging iron horseshoes or iron nails outside the doors and fences of the property will repel all Fay from the property, as will diverting running water, such as irrigation ditches, around the property. A full ritual cleansing/blessing of the property would also be advised. A ritual such as the strong house cleansing outlined in Part II would likely be successful.

To deal with phookas in their horse form, simply do not ride them. If a black pony with fierce yellow eyes walks near you, just keep walking. It also wouldn't hurt to carry an iron nail in your pocket to repel the creature. In some lore, creating a bridle containing three hairs from the phooka's tail will allow a person mastery over the phooka. However, this seems like far more trouble than it's worth—how would you get the three hairs in the first place? Better to just keep away.

Red-Cap

VITAL STATISTICS

Danger Level: 9

Rarity: 9

Difficulty of Removal: 9-10

Where Found: The borders of the Faery realm, the bowels of abandoned castles and ruined towers (particularly in Ireland and Scotland), any abandoned fort that has seen battle.

Common Symptoms: Small, leather-clad men with red caps seen, people receiving grievous injury in abandoned castles and forts.

LORE

Red-Caps are possibly the fiercest of all warrior Fay. They are the border guards for the world of Faery and are known to cause great harm to humans who cross their borders without an invitation. Their name and reputation are well-earned, for they dye their caps (hats) red with the blood of their enemies. In more gruesome tales, it is said that their caps will actually run with fresh blood during a battle, making the creatures appear even more ferocious and sending them into a frenzy. They typically appear as small, emaciated men with brown leathery skin. Though they are smaller than an average man, they are more than twice as strong. They often carry large scythes or spears as weapons. They wear worn leather armor and would never be without their signature red caps.

Red-Caps can be found patrolling the borders of the Faery realm and in abandoned buildings that have seen battle. The borders of Faery are often in secluded forest areas and are marked by things such as fairy rings (large circles of mushrooms often 6 to 12 feet in diameter), and fairy mounds (small hillocks with unusually lush vegetation). If you find yourself near one of these sites, it is best to treat it with great respect and leave the area, unless you have already had an introduction to the Fay that live there. If you have never treated with a faery before, do not start with a Red-Cap!

They are also found in ruined castles, towers, and forts. As befits their warrior nature, Red-Caps prefer to live in places that have seen battle and were once inhabited by warriors. They tend to be isolationists and are fiercely territorial. Once a Red-Cap has claimed a place for his own, he will defend it to the death from all comers, be they people, animals, or other Fay. However, if you are a professional warrior, such as a police officer or a member of the armed forces, he just might be willing to share if you can gain his respect. Such respect can only be gained by a show of martial prowess, usually by besting the Red-Cap in a fight. As Red-Caps are immortal warriors with centuries of experience, such an outcome is unlikely.

Red-Caps also have a maliciously mischievous side. Whereas they will do *anything* to keep intruders from the heart of their territory, on the edges they are sometimes satisfied with playing vicious tricks. On the edges of their home areas, they have been known to spook horses so that, their riders are thrown in dangerous terrain, or lure the unwary over cliffs or dead-falls. Once the human has been mortally wounded, the Red-Cap will then dip his cap in the fresh blood.

METHODS OF REMOVAL

If you encounter a Red-Cap while he is patrolling a border, the best thing to do is apologize, explain your mistake, and offer to leave immediately. Like most Fay, Red-Caps have a lot of pride and dignity and respond well to politeness and respect. If you disrespect either the Red-Cap or the area he protects, he is likely to attack—which never ends well for the human involved. As protection against such an encounter, it helps to carry cold iron. Of course, avoiding places that you suspect are home to the Fay is also a good idea. If you do find yourself in a fight with a Red-Cap, your only defense is a cold iron weapon or the protection of a higher force (Part II lists several common protective entities and how to ask for their aid). In some lore, reciting prayers or bible verses is believed to force the Red-Cap to flee.

If you encounter a Red-Cap in an abandoned building, the best things to do is, once again, apologize, explain that you were unaware he lived there, and offer to leave immediately. If you've just purchased such a property, then you will either need to bargain with the Red-Cap, which is inadvisable unless you're a professional warrior whom the Red-Cap might respect, or banish him. Because Red-Caps are so dangerous when angered, nothing but the strongest of banishing rituals will do. See Part II for a full banishing ritual. Thankfully, Red-Caps are extremely rare, especially outside of Britain.

The Wild Hunt

VITAL STATISTICS
Danger Level: 7
Rarity: 9
Difficulty of Removal: N/A
Where Found: Europe and North America.
Common Symptoms: Seeing or hearing a mass of spectral hunters.

LORE

Throughout Europe and parts of North America, stories are told of a group of spectral hunters that ride through the night. They may appear as horsemen in medieval armor accompanied by enormous hounds, antique soldiers from various ages, spectral cowboys, winged men, or hideous monsters. The hunt is also called the Slaugh in Ireland and the Ghost Riders in North America. In various stories, the Hunt is made up of faeries, souls of the restless dead, evil spirits, creatures of the underworld, or even gods led by Herne the Hunter.

All stories agree that the Wild Hunt in any of its guises is a fearsome sight. As to when the Hunt can ride, some stories say that it only rides on cold winter nights; others say they ride during storms; still others say they can ride on any night. The only thing all the lore agrees upon is that the Hunt only rides by night; never during the day. The Hunt is always large, consisting of dozens upon dozens of riders. In most stories, it rides through the air as a great spectral mass, although it has been known to ride on old country roads in near-corporeal form. In rural Sweden, it is believed that nothing can be constructed on old roads, lest the routes of the Hunt be obstructed and its riders angered.

The Hunt always spells bad luck for mortals who cross its path. In some stories, any mortal caught by the Hunt would be killed or compelled to join it for all eternity. A person can be caught by the Hunt by being ridden down, by being physically pulled onto the back of one of the horses, or by meeting the eyes of one of the riders. In other stories, the Hunt would only take up chosen targets, usually evil men. In such stories, the Hunt was often portrayed as a group of demons rounding up souls that had escaped from hell. In some more modern lore, a person who has suffered a great wrong, such as having a loved one killed or being violently betrayed, can call on the Wild Hunt to exact vengeance upon the person that wronged him or her by taking the offender up into the Hunt or sending him or her to hell. However, these stories are in the minority; in most lore it is impossible to have a positive interaction with the Hunt. In other stories, to even see the Hunt was bad luck. It would either herald some great calamity for the area in which it rode, or, at the least, the ruin or death of the beholder.

Methods of Removal

Once the Hunt has begun to ride, no power on earth can stop or dissuade it. The best we mere mortals can do is get out of its way and avert our eyes as it passes. The best defense against it is not to encounter it in the first place. Avoiding lonely roads in the dead of night is certainly the best way to avoid the Hunt. If you must travel at night through isolated or forested roads, saying a travel safety incantation, such as the one presented in Part II, before you set out may help.

In some lore, travelers who encounter the Hunt can avoid ill effects by getting out of its way and lying with their faces to the ground or covering their eyes. However, the effectiveness of such acts depends on the mood of the Hunt and may do no good at all. So, if you're traveling at night and hear what sounds like a great mass of riders, horns blowing, and hounds baying, run for cover.

Will-o'-the-Wisp

Faeries

VITAL STATISTICS
Danger Level: 2
Rarity: 4
Difficulty of Removal: 2
Where Found: Most commonly in swamps and marshes, occasionally in damp forests and fields, and more rarely in parks and backyard gardens.
Common Symptoms: Seeing unexplained balls of light low to the ground outdoors.

LORE

The Will-o'-the-Wisp is a type of faery seen all over the world, called by many names in different cultures: Faery Lights, Night Whispers, Hunky Punk, Teine Sith, Huckpoten, Irrbloss, Ruskaly, Corpse Candles, Ghost Lights, or Candelas. This faery appears as a small ball of shimmering light, usually 3 to 9 inches in diameter, hovering low to the ground with a green, blue, or white hue. Though they are most common in swamps and bogs, they have been seen in forests, parks, and backyard gardens.

Modern science has attempted to explain away Will-o'-the-Wisps as conflagrations of swamp gases and ball lightning. Though these scientific theories are reasonable explanations for some Will-o'-the-Wisp sightings, they do not explain all of them. Will-o'-the-Wisps can be distinguished from natural phenomena by their movement and their duration. Gases dissipate quickly, creating lights that only last for a few seconds, and their perceived movement is due to their expansion and dissipation. Will-o'-the-Wisp, on the other hand, can last for as long as they like, and are usually seen for several minutes at a time. Their movement is similar to that of flying insects; they dash to and fro and commonly circle objects, weave through branches, and go around obstacles.

Ball lightning is more difficult to distinguish from a Will-o'-the-Wisp. Such lightning can last for a few seconds or up to a minute or so, and has been known to move sideways, diagonally, and around or even through obstacles. However, it only occurs where there is a buildup of electricity, natural or otherwise, and is most common near thunderstorms. If you see a ball of light moving erratically, it may be ball lightning, but if you see it moving with intelligence, it is probably something more.

Normally, this faery is quite harmless and rather pretty to look at. However, some people find them so intriguing that they become almost entranced by them. The problem occurs when such an entranced person decides to get a closer look at the faery, and it begins to move away. While following the Will-o'-the-Wisp, due care is usually not taken in watching where one goes, and people have become trapped in bogs, fallen into holes or crevasses, and injured themselves or even perished. In some lore, the Will-o'-the-Wisp is simply a torch held by another mischievous faery, such as a phooka. The faery will use the light to lure people into marshes or forests and then deliberately extinguish the light, leaving the person lost and alone.

It is unclear whether the Will-o'-the-Wisp deliberately leads people onto dangerous ground or if it simply pays no attention to whether the area would be dangerous for humans. As such, it is either a trickster or merely amoral.

Methods of Removal

A person always has a choice whether to follow a Will-o'-the-Wisp and furthermore always has the option of watching where he or she is going. As a result, Will-o'-the-Wisps are not considered terribly dangerous and don't usually need to be removed. If you see a mysterious and beautiful light hanging low to the ground, just don't follow it.

If you are concerned that you might be entranced by a Will-o'-the-Wisp, look away as soon as you notice one and simply continue on your way. If you regularly pass an area frequented by Will-o'-the-Wisps, consider carrying a piece of cold iron, such as an iron nail from the hardware store, in your pocket when you pass by. This will make them avoid you and can neutralize any potential enchantment.

- 2 -

Bogeys are creatures of legend and lore that delight in frightening us. From the Black Ladies that snatch unwary children to the gremlins that reap destruction upon the unwary, they are storybook nightmares that lurk in the shadows, waiting for the chance leap out. Like many storybook monsters, bogeys need their victims to do something that opens themselves to attack; for example, Black Ladies only do harm to naughty, misbehaving children; gremlins are only truly dangerous when people fail to check and maintain technology; the Others have no place in this world unless someone opens a door for them; poltergeists are believed to be unknowingly created by people. Good boys and girls who pay attention and don't go dabbling where they know they shouldn't aren't likely to be bothered by bogeys. Right?

Black Lady

VITAL STATISTICS

Danger Level: 8

Rarity: 8

Difficulty of Removal: 5

Where Found: Sparsely populated rural areas, particularly in woods.

Common Symptoms: Children hearing a female voice calling to them out of the woods; naughty children disappearing during the night.

LORE

Black Ladies are a particular type of bogeyman known to steal incautious and naughty children during the night. In many countries, stories are told of unsavory women who live solitary lives deep in woodland areas and are suspected of loathsome activities, such as stealing children or practicing evil magick. Black Ladies are known to kidnap children who wander off into forbidden areas or deliberately misbehave. Depending on the version of the story told, the Black Lady may steal children to put in her stew pot, or perhaps only to use as a slave. Some famous Black Ladies are Black Annis of England, Baba Yaga of Russia, Callieach Bherea of Scotland, and even the unnamed witch from the Brothers Grimm story *Hansel and Gretel*.

One of the most well-known Black Ladies is Black Annis. Also known as Black Agnes, Black Annis is a blue-skinned bogey from English folklore said to haunt the countryside near Leicester. She appears as a haggard old woman with an emaciated body, stringy black hair, and sharp, talon-like fingernails. She also has only one eye. Like all such bogeys, she is said to haunt the countryside at night looking for naughty children to steal and devour.

Another famous Black Lady is Russia's Baba Yaga, also an old hag. She is believed to fly through the night, not on a broom, but in a mortar, using the pestle as a rudder. Her house is a log cabin deep in the forest, but instead of sitting on a normal foundation, Baba Yaga's house sits on a pair of chicken legs and can ambulate. Like other Black Ladies, she kidnaps and devours children who trespass on her land, particularly if they are rude or naughty. In some stories, gracious children who treat her with proper respect and obedience are spared and given great wisdom, though those kindly incidents are incredibly rare. More often, Baba Yaga can be bargained into releasing her prey if they can accomplish the tasks she sets to them—tasks that are impossible without magickal aid. However, in most stories Baba Yaga will simply devour the children she encounters.

Similar stories are common all around the world. All involve a woman, either an evil hag or a demented woman who has lost her own children, who will steal naughty children who do not go to bed on time, venture into forbidden areas, run away, or otherwise refuse to do as they are told. In almost all cases the woman is described as being quite ugly: old, blue skinned, deformed, emaciated, talon-nailed, and so on. Whether such stories were originally generated simply to scare children into doing what they were told or if they are based on something more sinister is uncertain. However, the stories are prevalent enough to warrant caution.

METHODS OF REMOVAL

In the stories, the only way for children to stay out of the clutches of a Black Lady is to do as they are told and behave as kind, loving children. Black Ladies do not steal children out of their beds, so there is little need to have any active protections against them. However, if a child is afraid of a Black Lady, then putting a protection charm of some sort in his or her room or on his or her person certainly won't hurt. Several protection charms that would be effective here are outlined in Part II.

In the unlikely event that an adult finds him- or herself in the clutches of a Black Lady, there are three things that can be done:

- ☆ First, an able-bodied adult can fight back physically. For this reason alone, adults rarely have encounters with bogeymen of any kind. Black Ladies are not known for enjoying fighting spirit in their victims, so physical self-defense is likely to be effective against most of them.

- ☆ The second defense against Black Ladies is to be unfailingly polite to them. The average Black Lady appears as a wizened crone, and, as such, is due the sort of respect one would give any elder.

- ☆ The third defense, of course, is to use protective magick. Magickal defenses should only be used against a Black Lady if you know that she means you harm and physical defenses have failed. In that case, personal shielding, such as that described in Part II is a good first step. Then, if necessary, forming an energy ball charged with "let me go" energy and throwing it at the Black Lady should distract her long enough for you to get away. (Instruction on the creation and use of energy balls is also detailed in Part II.)

Gremlin

VITAL STATISTICS

Danger Level: 3-6 (The danger posed by a gremlin depends entirely on what it breaks. If it breaks your alarm clock, then it's not so dangerous. If it severs the brake lines in your car, then you have a much bigger problem.)

Rarity: 5

Difficulty of Removal: 4

Where Found: Inside mechanical or electrical devices.

Common Symptoms: Inexplicable technical failures of mechanical or electrical devices.

Bogeys

Gremlins are a recent addition to the group "Things That Go Bump in the Night." Stories of gremlins originated with British airmen during the First World War. The airmen would explain mysterious technical failures in their planes and equipment as being caused by a mischievous outside force: gremlins. They are believed to be small, green, goblin-like creatures that cause mechanical or electrical failures. They are known for loosening bolts, breaking wires, tripping fuses, and causing computer crashes. Gremlins are to technical equipment what phooka and goblins are to farming. It is unclear whether the gremlin is a creature born of the 20th century or a much older creature that has successfully adapted itself to the modern world.

Though the first stories of gremlins were generated by the airmen of the Royal Air Force, they have since expanded their activity beyond aircraft to encompass all technical equipment. These days, gremlins can be found anywhere technology can be found—everywhere. Gremlins can do anything from causing gears to stick in a watch to creating hard-drive errors on your iPod. In the age of computers, everyone has experienced bizarre and unexplained failures of technical equipment. Such errors are probably the result of an errant piece of code in a program, but they might not always be. Gremlins are as at home in electrical devices such as laptops as they are in mechanical devices such as factory equipment.

Most of the technical failures caused by gremlins are mere annoyances. At their worst they might cause a flat tire on the way to an important meeting, or cause a computer to crash and erase several hours of unsaved work. More often they are likely to cause the television to turn off during a tense moment in a movie or make the fire alarm go off at 3 a.m. It is only in the movies that gremlins maliciously cause planes to fall out of the sky or brakes to fail on a deadly curve. Further, in the rare cases when gremlins do damage vital systems, proper maintenance and due diligence will usually discover the problem before it becomes a real danger. Gremlins are mischievous, not malevolent.

METHODS OF REMOVAL

The best way to deal with gremlins is to simply care for and perform regular maintenance on the technology in your life. That way their presence won't cause you any undue hardship. Gremlins are most likely to target the careless, so careful maintenance will also make them less likely to bother you.

For the magickally minded, simple blessings for technical devices are a good idea. These can be simple, such as saying something along the lines of "I bless you, new laptop. May your screen remain unscratched, your battery strong, and your circuits true." You may also try petitioning Ogun, a protective entity that specializes in technology, for aid. You can do so by saying something like: "O Great Ogun, hear me! I call upon you to protect my [piece of technology]. Please watch over and protect it." When the danger has passed, be sure to thank Ogun for his aid. It would be appropriate to verbally say *thank you* and possibly make some kind of offering, such as incense or food, in his name.

If the possible presence of gremlins worries you, simply do a basic cleansing ritual for the affected object or area. The Object Cleansing and Blessing detailed in Part II is ideal protection against gremlins.

You can also cleanse objects using energy balls. The basic process of creating and using energy balls is also detailed in Part II. To cleanse an object with an energy ball, simply create a ball of purifying energy that is slightly larger than the object being cleansed, and move the ball so that it encompasses the object. Then envision the purifying energy being absorbed by the object until it is cleansed and fresh. Then create another energy ball containing the kind of energy you would like the object to have, and let the object absorb that positive energy.

The Others

VITAL STATISTICS
Danger Level: 10
Rarity: 10
Difficulty of Removal: 10
Where Found: Cracks in reality or wherever summoned.
Common Symptoms: Insanity and death.

LORE

All cultures have their ultimate evil, their "that which must not be named." These are the creatures I call "the Others." These are creatures that must not be described, named, or even mentioned, lest such talk call them forth from wherever it is that they dwell. These are the creatures of nightmare, of deepest, darkest imaginings.

In most lore the Others do not live in this world but in alternate dimensions, places in between worlds, under the oceans, or even in far-off galaxies. They are described as anything from lurking shadows to monstrous giants. The one common feature is that something must be done in the here and now to summon these dread creatures from wherever it is they lie. In stories, those who attempt the summoning are usually insane or possessed, as no one in their right mind would summon such a creature. They are wholly malevolent, and their purposes are usually mass destruction of all life, enslavement of the planet, or turning it into a sort of hell dimension.

Thankfully, these creatures are the most rare of any featured in this guide. So rare in fact that they may or may not be real. The most well-known of these creatures, Cthulhu and Azathoth, are featured in the fictional works of H.P. Lovecraft, an early 20th-century horror writer.

His works have since taken on the sort of cult status that inspires fanatical devotion, to the point that some believe his works to be based on reality rather than a vivid, if twisted, imagination. But stories of these creatures are not limited to acknowledged works of fiction. Much ancient lore speaks of dread evil, whether it be in the form of an old god of a defeated nation or some terrible entity defeated by heroes of old that isn't quite fully dead, but sleeping. Are the Others real? Do you want to take the chance that they're not?

METHODS OF REMOVAL

As these creatures are not wholly of this world, they cannot simply come here and wreak havoc according to their will. They must be deliberately summoned here, usually by some particular, elaborate ritual. Preventing such summoning is by far the best way of dealing with these creatures. If you know who is attempting such a summoning, try to reason with them, if they're not insane. Rational people would only attempt this sort of ceremony as a joke, believing it to be fictional. In such cases, rational argument should dissuade them. Failing that, you can try to alter the ceremony. The ceremonies involved in such summonings are usually quite complex, requiring particular words to be spoken or particular artifacts to be used, and consequently are easy to derail.

If the ceremony being attempted looks like nothing more than ritual magick, try to stop it or put things out of order so that it won't work. If you think insane people are attempting something horrible, such as ritual sacrifice, call the police. Whenever you believe people are going to cause physical harm to other people, animals, or property, you *must* call the authorities. Do not endanger yourself unnecessarily. The police don't care why someone is committing a crime, only that it is being attempted or committed, and they will do everything in their considerable power to stop it.

If you are too late to stop the summoning, and it works, then you—and the rest of the world—are in serious trouble. Only the aid of a benevolent being of equal or greater power, such as the protective entities listed in Part II, will stop it.

Poltergeist

VITAL STATISTICS

Danger Level: 3-6

Rarity: 6

Difficulty of Removal: 4-5

Where Found: Everywhere

Common Symptoms: Objects being moved by unseen hands, knocking heard in the walls or on floors, doors slamming, lights turning on and off on their own, feeling of being watched, feeling of oppression.

LORE

Poltergeists, or "noisy ghosts," are the rarest and most controversial type of ghosts. This is due to the modern theory that poltergeist activity is not caused by a spirit at all, but by a living human being. Poltergeist activity consists of objects being moved by unseen hands, knockings heard in the walls or on floors, doors slamming, and lights turning on and off on their own. Because poltergeist activity is so overt (anyone and everyone can see it) it can be difficult, if not impossible to ignore. Poltergeist activity can also be very frightening; it is one of the only kinds of hauntings that can actually cause physical harm (usually from flying objects).

This kind of activity can be caused by an intelligent haunting, but that is fairly rare. When an intelligent ghost causes objects to move on their own or other poltergeist-like activity, it's usually for a reason—getting attention, preventing certain actions, and so on. Poltergeist activity, on the other hand, usually seems more random and is more persistent. Poltergeist activity may range from room to room, and may rapidly change from one type of phenomenon to another, such as from knocking on the walls to levitating objects. Poltergeists are also much more likely to create multiple types of phenomena at one time. Intelligent ghosts can do similar things, but usually only for a short time. Poltergeists seem to have the ability to cause spectacular phenomena for extended periods of time, such as making a bed rock back and forth for hours on end or making wild knocking sounds all night. Therefore if the phenomena are present only in short doses or when particular activities occur, then the cause is probably an intelligent ghost. If the phenomena persist over long periods of time and seem quite random, you are more likely to be dealing with a poltergeist.

Poltergeist activity is more commonly caused by a person living in the haunted area, usually without their being aware of doing anything. The person responsible is often an adolescent or young adult and usually emotionally troubled. Essentially, the person responsible exhibits bursts of unintentional psychokinesis (the ability to move objects with the mind). Several early 20th-century cases of poltergeist activity (knocking on walls, levitating objects, rains of stones on top of the house, and so on) centered around troubled young women. It was found that the activity only occurred when the young women were physically present, and the activity ceased when the young women resolved their emotional crises. Of course, this does not mean that poltergeist activity is limited to occurring around young women or even adolescents.

Poltergeist activity is also common around magickal practitioners who are still learning to control new magickal skills. Learning how to practice magick can open the mind to many things and can stimulate parts of the brain that do not normally get much use. It is possible that these previously unused parts of the brain create the poltergeist activity. Similarly, uncontrolled magickal abilities can send vast amounts of magickal energy into the area inhabited by the practitioner, causing all manner of unexplained phenomena. If you observe what might be poltergeist activity, the first thing to do is see if there are any young people around who might just be magickally gifted and don't know it yet, particularly if the poltergeist activity only occurs when that person is present.

However, as mentioned previously, not all poltergeist activity is caused by the living. Some rare instances of poltergeist activity do not involve a particular person always being present, and simply defy all other explanations. In these cases, a ghost, often that of a mischievous child, is the cause (for more information see the entry for intelligent ghosts). It is also possible for poltergeist-like activity to be caused by other metaphysical beings, such as goblins or boggarts. In those cases, look for other symptoms that might be evidence for the presence of those creatures.

METHODS OF REMOVAL

If the activity seems to be caused by a particular person, simply telling that person that he or she may be responsible can be enough to stop the activity. However, you must be very mindful of that person's feelings when you tell him or her. The person you think is responsible may have very strong beliefs that psychokinesis is wrong, or may be very upset to find that he or she was the one scaring the family. Also, you might be wrong. Just because it's *likely* that a particular person is responsible doesn't necessarily mean that he or she *is* responsible.

Offer to teach the responsible person how to ground and center (detailed in Chapter 7). This can do wonders for calming errant energy, stopping the activity, and even doing the person a world of good. If the responsible person is not open to learning how to ground and center, try to find out if there is anyone in his or her religious tradition to whom they should go.

If the activity does not seem to be caused by a person, then the spirit responsible can be banished and the location cleansed, as with an intelligent ghost.

-3-

Demons

The word *demon* has many different meanings; how it is defined often depends on one's religious background. Such theological questions shall not be addressed here, but whether they be servants of Satan or manifestations of the darkness in the human heart, demons are quite simply the embodiment of evil. Many mythologies speak of neutral or even benevolent beings that they call *demons*, and some branches of magick work with beings they call *demons* or *daemons*, but such beneficent beings are unlikely to cause you the sort of trouble this guide is designed to address, and, as such, will not be addressed here. For the purposes of this guide, demons are defined as malevolent metaphysical beings of indeterminate origins and often great power. The creatures that follow are some of the nastiest, foulest, and most dangerous creatures known to humankind.

Infernal

VITAL STATISTICS

Danger Level: 10
Rarity: 10
Difficulty of Removal: 9
Where Found: Everywhere, though most often where acts of evil have occurred.

Demons

Common Symptoms: Grave misfortune, feeling of intense dread/fear, scratches (particularly in groups of three), being physically struck by an unseen force, loud/startling unexplained sounds, very malevolent/violent unexplained phenomena, a feeling of being "taken over" by a malevolent outside force, frequent or repeating nightmares, an unexplainable foul stench.

LORE

Infernals are the most dangerous, and thankfully rarest metaphysical creatures known to us. They are noted as having varying appearances, and can appear as shadows, dark balls of energy, misshapen humanoids, or even very beautiful people. Further, some infernals are believed to be shape-shifters, able to shift their appearance to whatever best serves their goals. In many cases, infernals will not appear at all, because their work might be more easily done invisibly. They can also work through intermediaries via possession (see Chapter 6 for details). However, possession is possibly the rarest form of infernal work in this world, and, as such, you are unlikely to ever encounter it.

The presence of an infernal can be distinguished from that of other malevolent beings by the intensity of the negative phenomena experienced. Imps, ghosts, vampires, and many other beings can create a feeling of dread or heaviness in the atmosphere, but none can do so to the degree to which an infernal can. The difference can be likened to the level of darkness on a moonlit night compared to the pitch darkness of a deep cave—one is dark; the other is impenetrable. If the phenomena being experienced are annoying, slightly frightening, or mischievous, you are probably not dealing with an infernal. If the phenomena are intensely frightening, to the point of causing panic attacks or other physical symptoms, or are dangerous to life and limb, then you may be dealing with an infernal.

The presence of an infernal is most obvious to those who are metaphysically sensitive, to whom it feels unspeakably awful. Infernals give off the most negative and toxic energy imaginable; a sensitive in the presence of an infernal will "feel" the presence of this intense negativity and hatred. It can feel quite overwhelming, like being submerged in tar or buffeted by hurricane-force winds. Infernal energy will often make a sensitive feel nauseated and drained. Other negative entities feel malevolent to a sensitive, but infernals feel evil.

The biggest problem in identifying the presence of an infernal is that some spirits occasionally masquerade as infernals. Sometimes weaker spirits would like us to believe that they are powerful infernals so that we will fear them or do what they want us to. In such cases, the weaker being will do everything in its power to frighten, usually including manifesting loud sounds, scratching, or moving objects. The only way to know if the phenomena are caused by an infernal is to carefully look at the intensity of the phenomena (which can often only be diagnosed by someone experienced with malevolent phenomena), and for the particularly infernal, such as an intense foul stench at the time of the phenomena and scratches in groups of three. Although imposters are far more common than infernals, it is better to treat the situation as infernal to be safe—any technique that is effective against an infernal will almost certainly be effective against an imposter.

Not only do lesser creatures mimic infernals, but sometimes infernals will mimic the behavior of lesser creatures. The main theory as to why infernals would do this is in order to camouflage their true nature. Whereas a person is likely to go to extreme measures to rid oneself of an infernal presence, he or she is far less likely to do so if he or she thinks the infernal is only a ghost or imp. This would allow the infernal greater access to its intended target. One common theory is that infernals will pretend to be the ghosts of children in order to trick people into giving them permission to remain in their homes. Once that permission is given it is considerably more difficult to oust an infernal when it doesn't want to go. This is one argument for removing all uninvited metaphysical creatures from the home or workplace, even if they seem benign at first; it is so difficult to be certain what you're dealing with. Still, it is very difficult for an infernal to mask the malignancy of its presence, and someone skilled in sensing energies should be able to tell when a metaphysical presence is more than what it says it is.

METHODS OF REMOVAL

Prevention is the best way of approaching infernal problems. Infernals tend to target the weak and isolated: easy prey. The surest way to prevent an infernal from entering your life is to fill your life with strong benevolent energy. This role is most often filled by deities in various religions: God, Goddess, Kuan-Yin, Shango, and so on. Magickal practitioners who do not work with deities often fill this role with protective energies such as the elements, ancestor spirits, or created thoughtforms or egregores.

In the unlikely event that you or someone you know actually becomes the focus of an infernal's attention, you are going to need help. Dealing with infernals can be very dangerous and should not be attempted by an amateur unless there is absolutely no other option. If the affected person is of a religious background, contact a member of the clergy of his or her particular faith for a religious blessing or cleansing, as appropriate. If there is no religious preference, try to find an experienced magickal practitioner in your area that specializes in defensive magicks.

If you've tried everything and cannot find anyone to help you, you are probably in trouble. If it's possible to leave the area where the infernal manifests, you should do so. For example, if you strongly believe that an infernal lives in a barn near your home, don't go there. Consider moving. It sounds rather extreme, but the infernal is no laughing matter.

If you cannot remove yourself from the infernal—particularly if it has attached itself to you personally—there are a few things you can try. Burning purifying incense such as frankincense and myrrh, copal, or angelica can repel the demonic in general and infernals in particular, as can protective herbs such as rue, willow, angelica, and wormwood. The presence of strong protective amulets such as the cross, pentagram, or evil eye are also believed to repel the demonic and infernal. In such a case it would also be important to perform the strongest protection/cleansing ritual of which you are capable. This would be the time to explore the strong cleansings and banishings in the last chapter of Part II. If the presence of an infernal isn't an emergency, then nothing is.

Still, such efforts may or may not be effective depending on the strength of the infernal and the ability of the person performing the ritual. It is not unheard of for a poorly performed ritual to do nothing more than anger the infernal, making its behavior all the more dangerous. Once again, I urge you not to attempt to deal with an infernal without powerful and experienced aid.

Djinn

Demons

VITAL STATISTICS

Danger Level: 7

Rarity: 8

Difficulty of Removal: 8

Where Found: Deserts, particularly ruins. Places with high Middle Eastern emigrant populations.

Common Symptoms: Sudden sandstorms, prodigious shooting stars, a feeling of being unwelcome.

LORE

The Djinn are supernatural creatures of great power that originate in the deserts of the Middle East, and are most often found in the deserts there. They are known to spend time roaming the deserts, but they are most often spotted at the sites of ancient ruins that the desert has not yet swallowed. However, during modern times, they are believed to have followed émigrés from the Middle East out into the wider world.

Modern pop culture has turned the Djinn into the genie: the powerful but largely harmless wish-giver. The modern genie is often a spirit trapped in a lamp that must grant three wishes to anyone who possesses it. These genies are good-natured (or at least morally neutral), forced to do whatever their master wishes. The worst these modern genies do is interpret their master's wishes in unforeseen ways, often to punish their master's selfishness. Interesting as they are, the modern genie has little to do with its originator, the Djinn. The Djinn do not live in lamps, they do not grant wishes, and they are never, ever, slaves to anyone.

According to Arabic lore, the Djinn are a sovereign race of magick users unlike any other earthly creature. Unlike mundane creatures, the Djinn were not created from earth, or other natural elements. Instead, Allah created the Djinn from magick and smokeless fire, and because they were not made from the earth they do not inhabit the earth as we know it. Rather, they inhabit an alternate dimension connected to, but distinct from, mundane reality. Although they do not live here on a regular basis, the Djinn can and do travel to the corporeal world whenever they wish, though they have no real body here. As such, they are naturally invisible and can travel anywhere in the world almost instantly. Though they have no corporeal body, they can shape-shift to assume any appearance, though they have flaming eyes while in human form.

The one similarity between the modern genie and the true Djinn is that they both possess great magickal powers. Due to their otherworldly nature, Djinn can travel around the world instantaneously, giving them the ability to gather vast amounts of information so as to seem almost omniscient. This metaphysical nature also allows the Djinn to see and manipulate magickal energies and other unseen forces, which gives them abilities such as transfiguration, psychokinesis, and weather manipulation. In lore, Djinn most often demonstrate these abilities by creating showers of shooting stars, starting whirling sandstorms, and creating figures out of sand.

As with many creatures not truly of this world, the Djinn are morally neutral. They simply do not view the world in the same way that humans do, and thus cannot have the same moral values. Also, just as people can be, Djinn can be good, evil, or amoral according to their own natures and whims. Although most Djinn remain on their own plane and consistently ignore humans, some like to harass us in the manner of goblins—tripping us and getting us lost, out of what we can only assume is boredom. The Djinn who are most dangerous are those who make deals with evil magickal practitioners. Similar to most metaphysical creatures, Djinn have needs and desires that people can use to bargain with them for favors, such as gathering information or performing magickal tasks. Some of the less savory magickal practitioners will manipulate Djinn into doing great harm to their enemies. These are the Djinn that generally do the most harm to humans, and it's at the behest of other humans. Fortunately, or unfortunately for the evil practitioner, Djinn do not like being manipulated, and invoking their aid can have unforeseen and quite unpleasant consequences.

METHODS OF REMOVAL

The easiest way to protect oneself from Djinn is to be under the protection of a more powerful spirit or deity, such as those listed under Protective Entities in Part II. If one does not wish to invoke the protection of an outside entity, a protection charm would certainly be helpful, though the effectiveness of the charm would likely depend on the amount of faith the carrier had in it. (For examples of effective protection charms see Part II.)

Folklore tells of several ways to protect oneself from Djinn. Similar to many metaphysical creatures, Djinn abhor salt, and it can be used to create barriers they cannot cross. They also dislike loud sounds, pins and needles, knives, iron, steel, and silver. Common methods for keeping them at bay include sleeping with a knife under the bed, placing a silver coin in one's bathwater, and wearing a nail or metal ring on a string around the neck. It may also be helpful to burn benzoin incense or a combination of benzoin and wormwood to ward off Djinn. Carrying a mojo containing a silver coin, some wormwood, and a lump of benzoin would also be effective. (See "Tools" in Part II for complete instructions on the creation and use of mojos.)

Ghoul

VITAL STATISTICS

Danger Level: 5-8 (Most ghouls avoid confrontation and will run away from an able-bodied adult, making them mid to high on the danger scale of 1 to 10. However, should a ghoul turn and fight, it would become quite dangerous indeed.)

Rarity: 8

Difficulty of Removal: 8

Where Found: Cemeteries, morgues, fresh battlegrounds, and other places where human remains can be found.

Common Symptoms: Disturbed graves, the dying being hastened to their ends, desecration of the dead.

LORE

The ghoul, also called Ghul or Alghul, is a legendary creature originating in Arabic folklore that has since spread around the world. In the oldest lore, ghouls are scavengers who dwell in desert oases, feeding upon people and animals that perish due to the harsh desert conditions. In those older stories, they are little more than animals, having no real intellect and surviving solely on instinct. In more modern lore, they are best known for their tendency to dig up fresh graves and feast upon the recently deceased. In both modern and traditional lore, ghouls are nocturnal creatures that prefer secluded areas where they are safe from human interference.

Ghouls usually appear as humans, but with distinctive haunting eyes, talon-like fingernails, and sharp teeth. In some cases, they appear as rotting corpses, and in very rare circumstances they can appear to be indistinguishable from a normal person. It is unclear whether they are metaphysical creatures that were never human, revenants (see the entry on revenants for a complete description), or humans who have gone horribly, horribly wrong. In most lore, they are simple creatures of limited intelligence, but in others they have all the cunning of a human being. In most lore, ghouls simply haunt cemeteries in order to feast on the recently interred. In other lore, ghouls with a less ghoulish and more normal appearance will pretend to be doctors to the seriously ill or dying so that they can kill the patient and enjoy a still-warm meal.

In some Arabic lore, ghouls are created upon the death of a prostitute or other person who has shunned the rules of Islam. As with many other risen predators, the person who lives an evil or impure life is denied rest at the time of his or her death as punishment for his or her misdeeds. The restless spirit is then prey to evil influences and becomes a monster tormented with a hunger for human flesh. The ghoul then rises from the grave to seek sustenance, usually in the form of recently interred bodies. Such ghouls are almost always eating machines with the same intellect as the average scavenging animal.

Demons

Other tales, particularly those that use the term *Alghul*, state that ghouls were never human. Instead, they were evil spirits, and sometimes even disguised Djinn, who appear as humans in order to gain the confidence of and access to humans. These ghouls are portrayed as being very intelligent and cunning. They will often appear to be human women in order to lure untended children to their side, and the children are never seen again. Although such a ghoul appears quite human, it will usually have unusually pointed teeth. The Alghul is also known to lure solitary people into the desert by mimicking the cries of a traveler in distress, often leading the hapless into traps, waiting for them to die, and then eating them.

METHODS OF REMOVAL

In most lore, ghouls are scavengers, only eating the dead, thus rendering defense against them quite moot. In general, ghouls are cowardly creatures and will only fight if they have the advantage of numbers or if their intended victim is injured. When faced with an able-bodied adult or group of adults that recognizes them for what they are, they will usually flee. Ghouls would much rather their food didn't fight back. In some lore, they will also flee to their dens at the break of day. It is unclear whether ghouls are able to move about by day or if they simply prefer to move about at night.

Ghouls are tough adversaries. They are impervious to pain, have no need for breath, and have superhuman regenerative abilities and agility. As a result, they can be harmed by weapons, but usually not killed. A ghoul attack is not dissimilar to a zombie attack in a horror film. The ghoul will fight with nails and teeth, only stopping when it is physically unable to continue the attack—either because it is dead or no longer has limbs to move about with. To kill a ghoul its body must be virtually annihilated, and fire is the best weapon against one, though a shotgun would probably also be effective.

Hellhound

VITAL STATISTICS

Danger Level: 5-7

Rarity: 7

Difficulty of Removal: 7

Where Found: Anywhere, but most commonly near crossroads, lonely roads, and with the Wild Hunt.

Common Symptoms: Appearance of a large black dog with glowing red or yellow eyes, hearing the baying of an enormous dog.

Demons

A Hellhound is a large, black, supernatural dog. Some of the many Hellhounds found around the world are the Aufhocker, Grim, Bagat, Barghest, and Blood Dog. Hellhounds appear as unusually intelligent large black dogs with fierce glowing eyes—usually red or yellow. All Hellhounds have at least a few of the following characteristics: super strength, super speed, the ability to materialize and dematerialize at will, foul stench (particularly their breath), and possibly the ability to speak. In some lore, Hellhounds have corporeal bodies, whereas in others they are spectral, or some combination of the two.

Hellhounds serve several different functions in lore. In some lore, they are assigned as guardians of the underworld, graveyards, or even treasure troves. These Hellhounds are almost always unnaturally strong and vicious, being known to tear out the throats of anyone that threatens that which is guarded. Cerberus, the famous three-headed Hellhound of Greek mythology, stands guard at the entrance to the underworld, threatening to maim or devour anyone attempting to enter or leave illicitly. In other lore, Hellhounds are servants of underworld deities and are tasked with hunting down lost souls. This is true for the Hellhounds that are believed to run with the Wild Hunt. In the most gruesome tales, Hellhounds will hunt down the wicked and devour everything but their souls, which they take to the underworld.

Other Hellhounds have no master and simply haunt lonely roads and crossroads. These independent Hellhounds are some of the most frightening, because, unlike Hellhounds given specific tasks to perform, they cannot be avoided by being good and staying away from forbidden areas. For example, the German Aufhocker is a Hellhound that walks on its hind legs and leaps upon hapless travelers as they come upon crossroads. The Aufhocker does this for no apparent reason other than its own pleasure (or perhaps to feed). In some stories, the Aufhocker can shapeshift and will often leap on the back of its prey as a very small dog that grows in size and weight once the prey is on the ground. Thankfully, these vicious Hellhounds are seen far less often than their less dangerous counterparts.

One of the most common beliefs about Hellhounds is that their appearance is a portent of doom. In some lore, anyone who sees a Hellhound will either die or suffer great tragedy within days of seeing it, even from a distance. In England, the Barghest is a giant spectral dog that haunts those who are about to die. The Barghest will howl outside the home of the soon-to-be deceased, and has even been known to hasten that end by chasing its victims down lonely roads and frightening them to death. The most famous Barghest in English literature is Sir Arthur Conan Doyle's Hound of the Baskervilles, a famous opponent of Sherlock Holmes. In that story, the hound is believed to stalk members of the Baskerville family, running them down or frightening them to death as part of a curse. Such beliefs are quite common regarding all kinds of Hellhounds.

Even if the sight of a Hellhound does not portend death, it will portend misfortune, or, at the very least, entanglement with the supernatural. Hellhounds are not kind and gentle creatures; therefore, any encounter with them is likely to be perilous. They may cause grievous injury or simply frighten the person that sees them. When seeing a Hellhound is neither dangerous nor a portent of doom, it is often a portent of magick. Hellhounds are not often seen in modern times, but when they are seen, it is usually either in an area with intense magickal energy or by a magickal practitioner. In those circumstances, it is possible that the Hellhound acts as a warning to the practitioner that he or she needs to exercise particular care in his or her magickal dealings in the near future.

Methods of Removal

Most Hellhounds are frightening, but not intrinsically dangerous. Avoidance is the best course. Do not seek to cross a Hellhound that is guarding anything; don't attempt to cross its borders or steal its treasure. Hellhounds cannot be killed or injured by human weapons, and, in some lore, they are immortal and impervious to *any* kind of harm. Leave them alone.

For the more aggressive Hellhounds, the coming of the dawn is the only sure way to elude them. In some lore, blessed items or the tolling of church bells are also said to repel them. If you find yourself faced with an angry Hellhound, strong protection charms and the power of a protective spirit or two may help you to evade it until sunrise. (Charms and protective entities are more fully described in Part II.) However, if you are the specific target of an angry Hellhound, nothing less than divine intervention will save you.

Imp

VITAL STATISTICS
Danger Level: 2
Rarity: 2
Difficulty of Removal: 1-2
Where Found: Anywhere people spend time; most common in homes and places of work.
Common Symptoms: Feeling of dread/discomfort, feeling of being watched, a prickling sensation in the base of spine or abdomen.

LORE

Imps are small metaphysical creatures that seem to exist for no other reason than to upset people. They delight in scaring people by any means they can devise. Imps are invisible to most people most of the time, and it is unclear whether they have real corporeal bodies or if they exist as pure energy. However, when in the presence of those who are sensitive to astral energy, they appear as small balls of shadowy energy, or very small devils standing less than a foot tall, with brownish-red skin, pointy ears, and short tails. They are unpleasant and malevolent creatures. It is uncertain why they love to torment people, but it is possible that imps feed off the fear and negative energy their activities cause. Thankfully, however, they are not particularly dangerous.

Defense Against the Dark

In the Middle Ages, imps were often thought of as minor demons and familiars of witches. In this capacity, it was believed that imps would perform minor magics for their masters—usually those that involved harming others or causing chaos. Some lore tells of imps living within gemstones, talismans, or bottles so that their master could take them anywhere and always have their magic on hand. More often than not, the imps identified as witches' familiars were only everyday toads, lizards, and cats. Though it is possible that imps could serve others, most modern experience of them is as free creatures that serve only their own whims.

The presence of an imp can be recognized by feelings of vague discomfort and of being watched. The presence of an imp can also give a room a sense of heaviness or foreboding. Imps love to hide in closets and under beds, acting like monsters in a fairytale. They also love to follow you down a dark hallway, just for the sake of sending a shiver down your spine. They really do enjoy scaring people. For this reason, imps will sometimes mimic the lesser behaviors of more dangerous creatures such as goblins or demons, but imps can be distinguished from these more dangerous creatures by the physicality of their actions: Whereas more powerful creatures can do physical harm, imps can rarely manifest any real physical effects, simply creating high levels of fear without any physical basis. Another easy way to distinguish imps from more dangerous creatures is to observe the behavior of family pets. Cats and dogs have little to no fear of imps and will happily chase them down the hallway; however, more powerful creatures will usually scare pets silly. If your pet is unafraid, then you should be unafraid.

Imps are not particularly dangerous, just annoying. They cannot hurt you or even affect anything on the physical plane. An imp's presence is most disconcerting to people who are particularly sensitive to outside energies and are also unshielded. For unshielded sensitives, the presence of an imp may make them feel as though there's a dark shadow hanging over them. They may even feel a slight pricking sensation in the small of their backs. But for most people, the worst thing an imp can do is scare people so badly that they act irrationally and accidentally hurt themselves. Their presence can be uncomfortable, but if you keep your head about you, they cannot do you any harm.

METHODS OF REMOVAL

Imps are very easy to deal with. They are cowardly creatures and don't really want to fight. If you speak in a loud, firm voice and tell them to go away, they usually will. If you're in a public place, where talking to the air might be interpreted as crazy, simply visualize the imp in your mind (in whatever appearance seems right to you) and silently command it to leave you alone. Failing that, almost any display of magical power will scare it away. A good ritual house-cleansing is an excellent way to both scare off an imp and remove any negative residue it may have left behind. Both the basic and strong house cleansings in Part II would be effective against imps. Afterward, be sure to place a shield around the area to prevent the imp from returning.

Nachtmare

VITAL STATISTICS

Danger Level: 3-5 (The danger level of a Nachtmare depends on the intensity of the nightmares it creates and the physical health of its victim. The rarity corresponds to the danger level.)

Rarity: 3-5

Difficulty of Removal: 5

Where Found: Worldwide.

Common Symptoms: Intense nightmares, waking feeling drained, awakening in the night feeling a weight on the chest and being unable to move.

Lore

The Nachtmare is one of the more common malevolent creatures featured in this guide. Around the world, the Nachtmare is also called Old Hag, Uthikoloshe, and Mara. These creatures are essentially a form of vampire that feeds on people while they sleep. They are most often described as grotesque old women, squat goblin-like creatures, or an invisible weight on the chest.

Nachtmares enter the sleeping quarters of the living at night, their very presence causing the sleepers to have bad dreams. The Nachtmare will then either hover over its victim or sit on his or her chest and feed off his or her life essence. In some lore, the Nachtmare also feeds off the fear generated by the nightmares. After it's taken its fill, the Nachtmare will leave. When the victim wakes, he or she will feel drained or exhausted, and usually very upset by the nightmares, which are generally of truly terrifying intensity. In most cases, the victim will recover after a day or two, but in some very rare cases, the Nachtmare will drain its victim completely, and the victim never wakes up, or dies of fright.

No one is quite sure what exactly a Nachtmare is. Some believe that Nachtmares are malevolent metaphysical creatures that exist solely as a bane to humanity. Others believe that Nachtmares are a form of hungry ghost, a spirit of a deceased human that for some reason rises from the grave with a need to feed off the living. For example, the Mara of Scandinavia are believed to be the spirits of women who died unbaptized and therefore cannot rest. Whether they are purely metaphysical creatures or spirits of the unquiet dead, Nachtmares are undoubtedly unpleasant.

One of the common symptoms of Nachtmares is waking during in the night, feeling a heavy weight on the chest, and not being able to move. Modern science has named this phenomenon "sleep paralysis." It is common enough that most people experience it at least once during their lives. The theory is that during REM sleep, a person can partially wake, so that one's mind is mostly awake, but the parts of the brain that control motor function are still asleep. Interestingly, the phenomenon of sleep paralysis is also used to explain away claims of alien abduction.

Does this explain away the existence of Nachtmares? Better safe than sorry—take precautions as if you were dealing with a Nachtmare, but, of course, consult a physician if the symptoms persist.

METHODS OF REMOVAL

Although quite frightening, Nachtmares are not particularly robust and are rather lazy. Simple preventative protections, such as shielding or a sleep protection spell, will send them to seek easier prey. These same preventative measures, when preceded by a simple cleansing, will keep the Nachtmare from returning. All of these protective methods are detailed in Part II.

- 4 -

Vampires

Vampires are some of the most prevalent creatures in folklore from around the globe. From Dracula to the Acheri, every culture in the world has some kind of vampire deep in its lore. Some cultures so embraced the idea of vampirism that even their deities drink blood, such as Sekhmet of Ancient Egypt, Kali of India, and Tlaltecuhtli of Pre-Colombian Meso-America. For the purposes of this book, a vampire is defined as any creature that in some way feeds on human beings. This may mean feeding on energy (life force, sexual energy, chi) or blood. The vampire itself may be another person, a revenant, a metaphysical creature, or something heretofore unknown.

Several of the creatures from other sections of this book, such as hungry ghosts, can be considered vampires, but they are not listed in this chapter (see Chapter 5: Dead & Undead). Many creatures with vampiric characteristics also have characteristics that overlap with other categories of creatures. Here you will find creatures whose vampirism is their primary defining characteristic.

Classic Vampire

VITAL STATISTICS

Danger Level: 9

Rarity: 9

Difficulty of Removal: 5-9 (The difficulty of removal for a classic vampire depends on how determined the vampire is to have a particular person as prey and whether removal entails simply protecting the victim or destroying the vampire.)

Where Found: Everywhere.

Common Symptoms: Anemia, feeling drained after a good night's sleep, recurring nightmares, unexplainable puncture wounds.

LORE

The classic vampire is possibly the most popular monster in the world. Popular fiction has romanticized these creatures into daring heroes and seductive teen idols. Though it is great fun, such fiction ignores the heartless, and often repulsive killer of the world's folklore. Some of the many classic vampires in the world are the Blutsauger, Brahmaparush, Callicantzaro, Chiang-Shih, Craqueuhhe, Dearg-Dul, Kathakano, Kozlak, Krvopijac, Langsuir, Mandurugo, Moroi, Nelapsi, Owengu, Tlahuelpuchi, and Upyr.

A classic vampire is the creature most people think of when they hear the word *vampire*. These are humans, some living and some immortal undead, with supernatural powers, that feed off the blood and sometimes flesh of the living. In some lore, they are repulsive rotting corpses with no intelligence to speak of, and in others they have great cunning and the power to make themselves unspeakably beautiful and alluring. They are largely nocturnal, with some only being able to move about by night and others able to move in daylight at less than full strength. For example, the Blutsauger of Austria is an undead human with pale skin and an emaciated body that sleeps in its grave by day and hunts at night by preference, and is not harmed by sunlight. Though once human, the Blutsauger has almost no intelligence and is little more than a killing machine. In contrast, the Chiang-Shih of China are undead, but rise looking almost like a living human. However, they suffer from rigor mortis and have difficulty moving about. This effect lessens in time, and after a few months, they can move quite fluidly. Unlike the Blutsauger, the Chiang-Shih are solely nocturnal and possess great cunning, making them very dangerous indeed.

Classic vampires are made in several ways. In folklore, the most common reasons for someone to rise as a vampire are: improper burial, suicide, untimely death, or a wicked life. Such deaths make the spirits of the dead restless and therefore vulnerable to a sort of possession that makes them rise from the grave. For example, the Chiang-Shih are believed to be the risen victims of violent death, such as murder or suicide, and the Callicantzaro of Greece are believed to rise from the graves of those who were born during holy festivals and yet lived sinful lives. The Langsuir of Malaysia are born from women and children who died during childbirth. Essentially, any circumstance surrounding a person's death that might make it unlikely for them to rest easy could be a cause for them to return from the grave as a vampire.

The method of vampiric propagation most familiar to the modern reader is the idea of being bitten or somehow having one's blood infected with that of a vampire. Such infection may occur by simply tasting a vampire's blood or it may require repeated infections to ensure that the person becomes a vampire at the time of its death. In modern folklore, it is not uncommon for a person to require being bitten three successive times before being condemned to rise as a vampire upon death. Another common creation myth in modern vampire lore is that the victim must be drained of blood, almost to the point of death, and then be fed the blood of the vampire to immediately die and then rise again. These "modern" methods of vampire creation most differ from traditional methods in that the presence of another vampire is required. In traditional lore, anyone who dies under the wrong circumstances has the chance of becoming a vampire.

In all lore, classic vampires have supernatural powers, though the specific abilities vary from story to story. Most have superhuman strength, superhuman healing abilities, and superhuman senses of sight, smell, and hearing. For example, the Brahmaparush of India has superhuman strength and cunning, and the Kozlak of Dalmatia has telekinetic powers that allow it to cause poltergeist-like activity. Some classic vampires, such as the Moroi of Romania, have the ability to shape-shift or to control weather, particularly mists and fog. Some have the ability to hypnotize or enchant the living into allowing themselves to be bitten, sometimes repeatedly. Others are little more than normal people with a mania for the taste of blood.

No entry on classic vampires would be complete without mention of the most famous vampire of them all: Dracula. Though fictional, the Dracula story is what most people know about vampires. In Bram Stoker's tale, vampires are immortal seducers with abilities to control animals and storms, shape-shift, and hypnotize the living. When they feed, they can kill in a single bite, or take small amounts over time and turn their victim into a fellow vampire. Though this story is thoroughly fictional, the "Dracula vampires" are closer to the Moroi of folklore than they are to any other folkloric vampire.

In folklore, all classic vampires are evil; they kill and maim for sustenance and entertainment. The idea of the vampire as a debonaire and sympathetic character is a 20th-century invention.

METHODS OF REMOVAL

There are almost as many ways to repel vampires as there are stories about them. In many stories, vampires of all types are repelled by garlic and garlic flowers. This is because many cultures consider garlic to have the power to purify evil, making the root an anathema to evil's agents. In other lore, blessed items such as crosses (particularly those of silver) also repel vampires. In some lore, any blessing will do, whether the person using the blessed item believes in it or not, because it is the person who *gives* the blessing that imbues the item with power. Other tales require the person using the item to truly believe in it, as his or her faith is what actually keeps the monsters at bay.

In some lore, vampires cannot enter a home without permission. In stories such as Dracula's, this may be the permission of anyone already inside. In other stories, only the permission of a resident of the home will do. This never applies to public buildings. One explanation for this idea is that residences gain a sort of power if they are inhabited by loving families, creating a metaphysical threshold that acts as a barrier against any that would harm that family. However, many folkloric vampires can enter any building without an invitation, so it would be best not to rely on a threshold for safety.

One of the strangest threads common to many vampire legends is the idea that they are obsessive-compulsive counters. This belief gives rise to the following method of protection from vampires: strew small objects, such as rice or flax seeds, on the floor of one's bedroom or around the outer perimeter of one's home, and the vampire will be compelled to count every single one, delaying it until sunrise when they will be destroyed by the light. This odd belief is common in many disparate cultures, so maybe there's something to it.

Classic vampires can be killed, though it often requires rather drastic measures. In many stories, the resting place of the vampire must be approached during the day and the vampire must be staked through the heart. In some lore, this will kill it; in others it will merely pin the vampire to the coffin and prevent it from attacking (as with some revenant tales). If staking will not destroy it, then it can be beheaded, dismembered, burned (and its ashes scattered), or some combination thereof. Sometimes a classic vampire, such as a Brahmaparush, can only be destroyed through a ritual exorcism or by a holy warrior. Thankfully, such creatures are incredibly rare and you are very unlikely to meet one.

Modern Vampire

VITAL STATISTICS
Danger Level: 3-6
Rarity: 5
Difficulty of Removal: 8
Where Found: Everywhere.
Common Symptoms: Feeling tired/drained when in the presence of a particular person.

LORE

The modern vampire is a flesh-and-blood human being who, for whatever reason, either exhibits vampiric behavior or considers him- or herself to be a vampire. Vampiric behavior consists of (most obviously) drinking blood or in some way feeding off the energy of others. These modern vampires fall into four subcategories: Takers, psychic vampires, Sanguinarians, and Lifestylers.

All human beings potentially have the ability to take energy from others. In the same way that a magickal practitioner can learn to take energy from the natural world through the practice of magic, any person can (consciously or not) learn to take energy from other people. Some people are even born with this ability. The most important thing to remember when dealing with human energy-takers is that they are human beings just like you and me. Consequently, they must be treated with the same respect you would give to any other person.

TAKERS

Takers are people who, for various reasons, take energy from other people. Most people have run into a Taker at one time or another, though they may or may not have realized it at the time. If you've ever known someone who made you feel exhausted just be being around them—and we all have—chances are you've met a Taker.

Takers are not inherently evil. In fact, most of them don't even realize that they're causing any harm. These are people whose subconscious minds have learned how to tap into the energy of people around them. Because they are unaware of what they are doing, they have no control over whom they tap into or how much energy they take. They simply take from anyone who has the misfortune of being near them.

No one really knows why people become Takers. One theory is that the taking of energy begins when the new Taker goes through some type of trauma, either emotional, such as losing a loved one, or physical, such as becoming seriously ill. Extreme situations can drain new Takers of so much of their own energy that they need to take it from those around them, and they either consciously or unconsciously learn to do so. Usually, a person will stop taking energy from those around him or her once the trauma has passed. However, some people will continue taking energy, thus becoming Takers permanently.

Takers can usually be recognized by their outward behavior. They tend to be "drama queens." These are the people who always seem to be in crisis and always want to tell everyone who will listen. They crave attention and sympathy and will generally get quite upset if you refuse to commiserate with them. After being near them for too long, you will feel tired and irritable. Takers aren't usually all that dangerous as long as you can get away from them. They may drain some of your energy, but you will quickly recover once they go away.

Psychic Vampires

Psychic vampires differ from Takers in several respects. The most important distinction between a psychic vampire and a Taker is need. Takers do not need the energy they take, they just want it. True psychic vampires have an actual need for the energy they take. For whatever reason, psychic vampires are born lacking the ability to create certain types of energy that they need to function. They must take the energy from those around them in order to maintain their health.

Unawakened psychic vampires may not be aware that they lack this ability to create their own vital energies, and they are not aware that they are taking the energy they lack from others. Unawakened psychic vampires often have the same outward behavior as Takers and can be dealt with in the same ways. As with Takers, they are not truly dangerous because they don't take very much energy at any given time and recovery is swift.

Some psychic vampires are aware of their ability to take energy from others. For the most part, these people aren't a danger at all. Psychic vampires are *not* evil. Like any other human being, most of them are good people and won't take energy from others without their permission. The Sanguinarian and psychic vampire community is well aware of the potential dangers of feeding on the energy of others and has developed an ethical code they call the Black Veil to govern their actions. This code allows for the taking of energy only between healthy, consenting adults, and emphasizes respect for oneself and the community one lives in. Failing to follow this code will see a modern vampire blacklisted by the vampire community. There are an extremely rare few who will take energy from others without their permission.

Sanguinarians

Like psychic vampires, true Sanguinarians are people who require a particular energy signature that they do not produce and must obtain from outside sources. Unlike psychic vampires, Sanguinarians absorb this energy by physically consuming human blood from willing donors, often called Black Swans. The amount of blood that Sanguinarians consume is very small, and, when donated in a safe, sane, and hygienic manner, poses no danger to the health of the donor. Unlike classic vampires, Sanguinarians are normal human beings that get up and go to work in the morning like the rest of us. Like psychic vampires, Sanguinarians generally follow the Black Veil code of ethics and are no more dangerous than any other kind of person. In fact, they are often more conscious of their behavior than others because behaving badly is not conducive to finding or keeping willing donors.

Lifestylers

Lifestylers are not true vampires, but they often call themselves such. A Lifestyler is someone who enjoys the energy and ambiance of the vampire community and will often participate in it. They may or may not choose to drink blood or feed on energy, but if they do, it is only a choice and not a requirement. Some Lifestylers will call themselves vampires either because they do not fully understand what it means, or because they simply enjoy the feeling it gives them. You will often find Lifestylers in Goth- or vampire-themed clubs or other places where Sanguinarians or psychic vampires congregate.

METHODS OF REMOVAL
Takers

Basic shielding will protect you from the short-term effects of being near a Taker. However, shielding alone can be insufficient if the Taker turns his or her attentions toward you. If the Taker tries to get you involved with his or her never-ending crises, simply refuse to do so and walk away. By steadily refusing to give them the attention they want, they will usually move on to a more willing audience.

The best way to deal with Takers is to simply not be around them. If you cannot physically get away from a Taker (if the Taker is a classmate or a coworker), the best thing to do is spend as little time talking to them as possible. This minimizes the Taker's opportunities to monopolize your attentions and therefore energies.

Psychic Vampires

Basic shielding and avoidance will usually be sufficient to keep you safe from any negative effects created by unawakened psychic vampires. For the most part, awakened psychic vampires are not a threat to anyone, as they are governed by quite stringent ethical rules. However, if you believe you are being attacked by a purposeful and malevolent psychic vampire, you will need to perform a hex-breaking ritual. The Elemental hex-breaking ritual presented in Part II should be sufficient in most situations. Though an attack by a psychic vampire is not a curse or hex, the method of removal is the same. The hex-breaking will sever the metaphysical connection between the vampire and the victim, cleanse the negative effects, and reestablish strong shielding to prevent further negative effects.

Sanguinarians

There is little need for magickal protection against Sanguinarians because they feed physically. If you don't want to be a donor, don't offer. In the incredibly unlikely event that a living, breathing human being tries to feed on your blood without permission, scream and call the police—you're dealing with a psychopath (who is likely not a real Sanguinarian).

Lifestylers

Lifestylers are only a danger to others when they are also Takers or if they are physically violent. If you think someone is a Lifestyler and a Taker, follow the protective steps outlined previously for Takers. If you think a Lifestyler poses a physical threat to you, use your common sense and do what you'd do when threatened by any other person: run away, get help, and call the police if necessary.

Sexual Vampire

VITAL STATISTICS
Danger Level: 8
Rarity: 8
Difficulty of Removal: 7
Where Found: Populated areas.
Common Symptoms: Exhaustion after intense dreams, nightly visitations of obvious nature.

LORE

The sexual vampire is a supernatural creature who feeds on the sexual energy of humans. Some examples are the Chedipe, Dames Blanches, Feu Follet, Ghaddar, Liderc Nadaly, Inkubus, and Succubus. Almost universally, these creatures appear to their victims as the most exquisitely beautiful men and women imaginable. On the rare occasions that they do not appear so, they are invisible. Though they usually appear human, many believe that this is an illusion put on to help secure potential victims. Some sexual vampires are believed to have batwings, horns, or talon-like feet in their natural state.

The behavior of many sexual vampires is similar to that of the Leanan-sidhe covered earlier. They will appear to a potential victim as a beautiful and alluring human and thoroughly seduce him or her. The vampire will then lead its prey to a secluded spot to engage in sexual activity. The sexual vampire will then feed off the sexual energy released by its prey. These activities will go on until the sexual vampire is sated, the victim dies, or they are discovered by others—although sexual vampires are generous with their favors, they seem to abhor an audience. Those that survive such an encounter will often fall ill afterward due to sheer fatigue.

If the victim is lucky, he or she will recover after a day or two in bed. If the victim is unlucky, he or she may get the flu, pneumonia, or suffer from constant fatigue for the rest of his or her life.

In some lore, these vampires visit their prey late at night, often while they sleep. The vampires have their way with their victims, feeding off their lust and sexual energy. To the victim, the visitation may seem like a very intense dream, or he or she may be more fully aware of what's happening. Often such visitations will be repeated night after night until the victim begins to waste away. In such a way, it is even possible for the victim to be loved to death. The greatest danger of this kind of sexual vampire is that its method of feeding is often so pleasurable for its victims that the victims allow or even encourage them to return, and rarely seek help in preventing further attacks.

Other lore depicts sexual vampires as being rather more monstrous in their behavior. In these stories, like the Chedipe of India, they appear as beautiful people and entice their victims into secluded spots where they incite their victim's lust and then physically devour them during intercourse, rather like a praying mantis. The Ghaddar of Northeast Africa lures unsuspecting men into seclusion and then devours their genitals while they still live. The victims of these sexual vampires never survive the encounter.

METHODS OF REMOVAL

Sexual vampires of any kind are extremely dangerous and should be avoided if at all possible. Their greatest weapon is seduction, and your greatest defense is to simply not be seduced. If an absurdly beautiful person whom you don't know and whom no one you trust can vouch for attempts to seduce you, gather your willpower and say no. If he or she is really interested, you'll get a call later; if he or she is not really interested or is a monster, then you're better off without.

Nocturnal visitations by sexual vampires can be prevented with proper wards on your dwelling. Such wards can easily be created by the protective elements of a house cleansing ritual or a sleep safety spell, both of which are detailed in Part II. If you have already been visited by a sexual vampire, it would be wise to do a personal hex-breaking, such as the

Vampires

Elemental hex-breaking, to break the vampire's ties to you before the protection ritual in order to ensure its effectiveness. These methods will only succeed if the victim truly does not want to be visited.

VITAL STATISTICS
Danger Level: 9
Rarity: 9
Difficulty of Removal: 7
Where Found: Common in places of dense population and poor sanitation, near burial mounds.
Common Symptoms: Occurrences of highly contagious wasting sickness or plague.

LORE

Nosferatu are a kind of vampire who feeds on the energy or life force of a human being and spreads disease. The disease will quickly spread through a village or town, killing large swaths of the population. Some other examples of this type of creature are the Acheri, Anito, Cihuateteo, Lampire, and Neunter. They have a varied appearance and can look like anything from a human child to a rotting corpse. In some lore they appear as floating balls of light, much like a Will-o'-the-Wisp, or they may be totally invisible. The only consistent indication of the presence of a Nosferatu is unexplained and highly contagious illness. But unlike natural diseases, there will be no apparent cause for the wasting disease caused by Nosferatu. For example, a natural disease often has a traceable "patient zero," the person who carried the disease into the affected area. In the case of Nosferatu-spread disease, many people may be affected at once, sometimes having no connection whatsoever. It is often very difficult to determine whether a plague is caused by a Nosferatu or natural causes without investigation by a medical expert.

It is unclear why Nosferatu spread disease in areas where they feed, rather than just feeding. One theory is that Nosferatu cause disease in order to create intense emotions of pain, despair, and grief. It is certainly true that seemingly incurable disease causes despair and grief in both the infected and their loved ones. Once these intense emotions are present, the Nosferatu can feast until it is truly sated. It is also possible that the creatures may do it for the malevolent joy of doing harm. Either way, the presence of a Nosferatu causes great harm to everyone in the affected area.

Nosferatu are not malevolent beings from other planes; they are spirits of the unquiet dead. In some lore, such as that of the German Neunter, Nosferatu are the spirits of those who were gluttonous or maliciously selfish in life and consequently rise to satisfy that hunger after death. In other stories, such as that of the Mexican Cihuateteo, they are the angry ghosts of women and children who died during childbirth that inflict sickness on others in anger from their untimely deaths. Others, such as the Anito of the Philippines, are spirits of the dead who use the spread of disease to prevent the desecration of their graves. Nosferatu who use disease to protect their graves will only infect those who come near their burial place, unlike other Nosferatu who roam large areas infecting anyone they find.

Once relatively common, stories of this kind of vampire have since grown rare. Whether this is due to fewer Nosferatu being in the world or the spread of modern medicine is uncertain.

METHODS OF REMOVAL

There are several ways of dealing with Nosferatu. The most effective way to prevent infection by a Nosferatu is to practice scrupulous hygiene when dealing with the sick and to use strong shields. The basics of shielding are covered in Part II. Personal shields create a barrier that evil should not be able to cross, making it difficult—nigh unto impossible—to be affected by a Nosferatu. In India, it is believed that red thread, woven into a bracelet or charm, will ward off the effects of a Nosferatu and keep the wearer safe. Other kinds of personal protection charms will likely be equally effective. Also, behaving respectfully and stating that you mean no harm to any graves while walking through burial grounds can't hurt.

Vampires

As mentioned in the entry on classic vampires, garlic is excellent for warding off all kinds of vampires. Garlic has excellent purifying and cleansing qualities. Modern natural medicine lauds the many health benefits of consuming garlic and its curative abilities. Such a commonly available healing and purifying plant should not be ignored when dealing with Nosferatu. Carrying a clove of garlic in one's pocket, wearing a bunch of garlic flowers, or simply consuming lots of garlic should all be effective at repelling Nosferatu and negating their effects.

Vampire Witch

VITAL STATISTICS
Danger Level: 8
Rarity: 9
Difficulty of Removal: 5-8
Where Found: Worldwide.
Common Symptoms: Feeling drained or complaining of a mysterious wasting sickness, mysterious blood loss overnight.

LORE

The vampire witch is another common monster across many cultures, going by names such as Abchanchu, Adze, Asema, Bebarlang, Chonchon, Jigarkhwar, Obayifo, and Tlacique. These are magickal practitioners gone terribly wrong. These nightmarish folk have rather spectacular powers and use them to spectacularly malevolent ends. They either astrally project or shape-shift and go to their victims to feed on their life essence or their blood.

The Bebarlang of the Philippines is an example of the astrally projecting vampire witch. These practitioners have mastered the art of astral projection and will travel, alone or with others of their kind, to the homes of their enemies late at night and feed off of their life essences. (For a brief description of astral projection, see the entry on living ghosts.) Persons so attacked wake feeling drained and often having had bad dreams. If such feedings are repeated often enough, the victim can fall ill or even die.

Similar to the astral-projecting type, there are several vampire witches who travel in the form of a Will-o'-the-Wisp—a ball of fiery light, often blue or green in color. (For a more lengthy description see the entry on Will-o'-the-Wisp.) The Tlacique of Mexico and Obayifo of West Africa will physically transform themselves into Will-o'-the-Wisps and travel to their victims in order to drink their blood. The vampire will often scratch or bite the victim while he or she sleeps, taking only small amounts of blood at any one time. The Tlacique does this in order to absorb the power of its enemies or to take vengeance upon them. The Obayifo does so in order to extort money from villages, threatening to attack the village if it is not paid off.

The rarest type of vampire witches will physically transform into beasts in order to feed off the blood of the living. The Chonchon of South America transform into human-headed vultures in order to feed. Such a form strikes terror in potential victims and gives the vampire excellent mobility. Unlike astrally projecting or Will-o'-the-Wisp vampire witches, those that transform into beasts attack while their victims are awake and aware, making them by far the boldest of the vampire witches.

In many cases, the astrally projected or shape-shifted vampire uses that alternate form as a means of accessing its victims without detection. For example, the Adze of Togo shape-shift into the forms of flies, mosquitoes, or other small flying insects in order to gain undetected access to their victims. Such a form is far less glamorous than shape-shifting into a lion, but it's also far less likely to arouse the awareness of anyone standing guard. In other cases, the vampire will use its alternate form to gain the strength and speed necessary to survive any confrontation with its enemies. The Asema of the Caribbean is one such vampire. It takes the form of a ball of fiery blue light and then strikes its victims like a lightning bolt, feeding while they're stunned. Though it is terribly unsubtle, the Asema cannot be physically injured while in its shifted form.

Vampires

METHODS OF REMOVAL

Most of the astrally projecting and Will-o'-the-Wisp vampire witches can be kept away with simple protection rituals or charms. Any protective efforts that create a psychic barrier should keep these creatures out. For the Bebarlang, lore details that they can only be kept away by a talisman made from pieces of the victim. One must mix a few drops of blood, some hair, and a few fingernail parings with wax and fashion it into a human or angelic figure. This can either be placed near a person while he or she sleeps, or be worn on a cord around the neck.

For those vampire witches who transform into beasts, more drastic measures must be taken. Magickally, the best measure that can be taken is to call on a more powerful being for protection. Or, if you know the attack is coming, you can prepare war water and throw it on the beast. (For detailed instructions on how to create war water, see Part II.) Of course, whenever you are under physical attack, take common-sense physical protective measures. Running away and calling for help are very good ideas under these unlikely circumstances.

− 5 −

Dead and Undead

The living have always feared—and been fascinated by—the dead. Cultures all around the world have created vast and complex funerary rites to assure that the dead move on rather than remain to haunt the living. Festivals such as Halloween, Samhain, Dia de los Muertos, O-bon, Ching Ming, and many others are celebrated in various countries to appease and pay homage to the dead so that they will bring blessings rather than plagues to the living.

But sometimes funerary rituals are not performed, ancestors are forgotten, and the dead are disrespected. This can make them rather testy, and that is when they become a problem. When the dead do not rest quietly, they can be seen in several forms. In this chapter, we will explore several of the myriad types of ghosts often seen in the world, as well as revenants and shadow people.

Revenants and shadow people are straightforward enough to be left until their respective entries, but ghosts require a little more of an introduction. Many different theories attempt to explain ghosts—there is probably one for every person who's ever contemplated the question.

So before getting to specific types of ghosts, I will outline a few of the most common theories, beginning with the mundane and moving on to the metaphysical.

MISIDENTIFICATION OF NATURAL PHENOMENA

The theory most often cited by those who do not believe in ghosts is that they are nothing more than the misidentification of natural phenomena. This theory states that there is no such thing as ghosts, and the ghostly phenomena observed by believers have perfectly logical, mundane explanations. Under this theory, a banging sound in the hallway is likely to be bad plumbing or the natural settling of a house, rather than a spirit or magickal being. This theory does not suggest that people who think a ghost is present are lying or making things up, but only that they are mistaken.

Although this theory seems harshly skeptical, it is actually a good first theory when dealing with ghostly phenomena. When experiencing something they cannot explain, some people will immediately jump to the conclusion that ghosts must be the cause, but more often than not, a strange bump in the night does indeed have a reasonable, mundane cause, and it is always wise to check for such a cause before moving on to investigate the possible paranormal aspects of a situation.

HOAX

Another common mundane theory is that ghostly phenomena are the product of a hoax: someone deliberately causing the phenomena to make it look paranormal. In some cases, the hoax may be a relatively harmless prank, such as hiding in the bushes and making scary noises. In other cases the hoax may be an elaborate staging designed to make people believe a location is haunted (often for the purposes of marketing).

One of the most famous ghost hoaxes is the story of the "Amityville Horror." You may be familiar with the book or movies that tell the supposedly true story of the violent haunting of a Long Island home. For years, people across the country believed that the story was true, and it wasn't until relatively recently that the parties alleging the haunting admitted that they made the whole thing up and had never experienced paranormal activity in the home. Of course, this wasn't until they had made thousands of dollars from books, films, and other merchandise.

More often than not, people who admit to experiencing ghostly phenomena truly believe what they are saying. However, some people may perpetrate a hoax to get attention, and you always have to be cautious when there's money to be made. Hoaxes are fairly rare, but it's always a possibility.

Hallucination

A hallucination is the experience of a physical occurrence without any outside stimuli—essentially: seeing, hearing, or smelling something that isn't really there. There are those who believe that many of the people who experience ghostly phenomena are simply "seeing things."

Although this is a convenient way of explaining away ghostly phenomena, it simply cannot account for the sheer number of ghost sightings that occur. It is believed that as many as one out of every three people experiences a ghost sighting. However, it is believed that only one out of every 10 people ever experiences hallucinations. It is certainly possible that some experiences of ghostly phenomena are, in fact, hallucinations, but not all of them.

Psychosomatic Construct

A more interesting mundane theory for explaining ghostly phenomena is the idea of psychosomatic constructs, which are basically phenomena caused by the mind. Essentially, under this theory, ghostly phenomena are manifested by the people experiencing them. For example, people who experience the death of a loved one may want to see that person so badly that their minds will in fact "see" him or her there.

This theory is a common explanation for poltergeist activity (ghostly phenomena that moves objects and causes loud noises; for more information see the entry in Chapter 2 on poltergeists). The idea is that some people, often adolescents or people with untrained magickal talents, have the ability to manifest ghostly phenomena without realizing it. These people then think they're being haunted.

Of the mundane theories, this is one of the most plausible. People often see what they expect or want to see, so it is not unreasonable to believe that some experiences of ghostly phenomena are actually caused by the minds of those experiencing them.

ENERGETIC MEMORIES

Under the theory of energetic memories, the first of our metaphysical theories, some types of ghostly phenomena are caused by the residual energy of past events. The basic idea is that places (such as buildings or natural locations) absorb energy and hold it. That energy is then released through time, causing echoes from the past to be experienced in the present.

This theory is one of the more common explanations for residual hauntings. A residual haunting is an experience of the same ghostly phenomena over and over again at specific intervals; for example, seeing a figure move down the hall every Wednesday at 10 p.m., or soldiers fighting on an old battlefield.

TIME SLIP

Another theory sometimes used to explain residual hauntings is the idea of the time slip. A time slip is when a person manages, somehow, to slip momentarily from one time period to another. Under this theory, when people see a ghostly figure, what they are actually seeing is someone from another time (past or future) who has "slipped" into the present. However, the person who has "slipped" into the present may not be fully here, which may account for the fact that some ghostly apparitions don't seem to notice those of us here in the present.

This theory can also account for why, sometimes, when people go into older buildings, they may see a flash of things that occurred there in the past or will occur in the future. Under these circumstances, it would be the person from the present slipping into the future or past. Perhaps someone from the past would then see the person from the present and think him or her a ghost!

Dead and Undead

DECEASED HUMANS

By far the most prevalent theory for explaining ghostly phenomena is that they are the presence of deceased humans who, for whatever reason, remain on this plane of existence. There are many theories as to why a spirit of a human would remain on this plane after death, and equally as many for how they manifest to the living. We will explore only a few of those theories here.

IMPRINT

An imprint is a part of a deceased person that manifests as ghostly phenomena without that deceased person being aware of it. Under this theory, some part of the energetic body (aura, spirit, soul, or whatever you choose to call it) of a deceased person manifests in the present and causes ghostly phenomena. This is essentially the same idea as the theory of energetic residue, except it refers solely to the manifestation of human energy and not other kinds of energy.

BETWIXT AND BETWEEN

Some people believe that ghosts are either half in this world and half in the next, or wholly in this world. Under this theory, ghosts may be here because they have refused to move on, or they may be "stuck" here. This may be because the ghosts have unfinished business on this plane or because they have yet to realize they're dead. For whatever reason, under this theory, ghosts are spirits of the dead who have yet to fully move on to whatever lies beyond this life.

SELF-AWARE SPIRIT

A self-aware spirit is a human personality that remains intact after death and is able to interact with the world of the living. When most people think of a ghost they think of a self-aware spirit. Such a ghost can appear as a figure, move objects, speak, and appear or disappear at will. Just about any kind of ghostly phenomena can be ascribed to the work of a self-aware spirit, and often are.

TELEPATHY

An interesting theory as to how ghosts manifest to the living is based on telepathy. The theory states that when a person experiences ghostly phenomena, he or she is not actually experiencing physical phenomena. Instead, the ghost that is trying to communicate with the living telepathically sends information that our brains interpret as ghostly phenomena. For example, when someone sees the figure of a person before her, instead of the eyes perceiving the figure and sending signals to the brain, what is actually happening is that the ghost is sending information directly to the brain of the living person that says that a figure is before her, bypassing the eyes.

This is an interesting theory that could explain why two people can be looking at the same spot and only one might see the ghost there. The person seeing the ghost could simply be stronger telepathically and therefore better able to receive the information the ghost sends. However, this would not explain the numerous instances of ghostly phenomena being caught on film or audiotapes.

OTHER METAPHYSICAL BEINGS

Some people believe that *any* "unnatural" phenomena they experience *must* be caused by ghosts. But as the length of this book can attest, that is untrue. It is important to realize that ghosts are not the only things that can go bump in the night. If your jewelry keeps disappearing off the nightstand, you are as likely to be dealing with faeries or imps as with ghosts.

It can be very difficult to determine whether particular unexplained phenomena are likely caused by ghosts or some other kind of being. Often, the best way to find out is to simply go to the location where the ghostly phenomena is occurring and ask whatever is present to identify itself.

Another way is to look at the totality of the circumstances: Most metaphysical beings have particular things they do, and other things they simply don't do. For example, an imp may create feelings of foreboding or move objects, but is extremely unlikely to speak or do anything that can be perceived as being beneficial. If several phenomena have occurred, look to see if there are any emerging patterns. If shiny things keep disappearing, you likely have faeries on your hands. If you keep hearing a disembodied voice that asks for something, you're likely dealing with a ghost. Unfortunately, there is no fool-proof way of identifying what you're dealing with except hard-won experience.

Hungry Ghost

VITAL STATISTICS

Danger Level: 7
Rarity: 7
Difficulty of Removal: 5-6
Where Found: Everywhere.
Common Symptoms: Wailing heard at night, figures beckoning the living out into the night, people being found drained of life.

LORE

Hungry ghosts are a type of ghost that preys upon the living in order to feed, seek revenge, or make up for some loss in life. Some such ghosts are the Gaki, La Llorona, Angiak, Baka, Bakechochin, Bloody Mary, Buruburu, Eretiku, Kindermörderinn, Masan, Pret, Strigoi, and Vodnik. Such ghosts are said to be the spirits either of evil people, such as murderers or the greedy, or those who were wronged in life, such as women who lost their children, children who died at birth, murder victims, and the like. For whatever reason, these ghosts have a terrible hunger that must be assuaged either by feeding on or tormenting the living night after night.

Hungry ghosts are quite possibly the most dangerous ghosts in existence. These ghosts, by their very definition, attack the living. Some, such as the Gaki of Japan, call out to the living, making the sounds of an injured person or a child calling for help. But once the Good Samaritan finds the source of the cries the ghost will attack, either siphoning off the person's life force or drinking the person's blood. The Gaki is believed to be the spirit of an evil person, tormented with an unquenchable thirst for life or blood as punishment for their evil deeds in life. Other life-draining hungry ghosts are believed to be the spirits of those who were improperly buried or those whose graves had been desecrated. Such ghosts rise from their graves to punish those who failed to give them proper respect in death.

Other hungry ghosts, such as the Radiant Boys, are vengeance ghosts. These ghosts rise from the grave for the specific purpose of finding the persons who wronged them in life and punishing them. Unlike other hungry ghosts, those bent on vengeance will permanently return to their graves once they have been avenged. According to German legend, the Radiant Boys are the ghosts of young children who were murdered by their own mothers. They are believed to torment their still-living mother with vicious poltergeist-like activity until the mother goes mad or does herself harm. In lore, it is common for these vengeance ghosts to chase those who have wronged them down lonely paths and roads. In more modern stories, they have been known to chase cars, frightening the driver so much that the car runs off the road.

Still, other hungry ghosts are tormented by a need to fill some loss they incurred before death. These are often the spirits of people who were robbed of a precious item, such as a family heirloom, immediately before death, or those who caused a great harm immediately before death and are wracked with guilt. Such a spirit is La Llorona, the Weeping Woman. Almost every country in Latin America has a story similar to that of La Llorona, a tale of a woman who drowns her child in a river in a fit of jealousy. Within days, she withers and dies due to remorse. Her ghost is then doomed to forever walk the river bank, looking for her child. This ghost is dangerous because it can no longer tell the difference between her child and any other that might walk untended near the river at night, and she has been known to snatch unwary children away. These hungry ghosts will look for whatever it was they lost and try to take anything that resembles it. Though this kind of hungry ghost isn't truly malevolent, its lack of care in what it takes makes it quite dangerous.

METHODS OF REMOVAL

Thankfully, these ghosts are quite rare and are usually easily dealt with. Most hungry ghosts are repelled by normal magickal protections such as shielding or a protective or blessed charm. Information on both shields and protective charms is detailed in Part II. Such basic protection should keep a hungry ghost from targeting you for attack.

If you find yourself under attack from a hungry ghost, your defense depends on whether you are a random victim or if you wronged said ghost. If you are a random victim, a standard protective incantation should force the ghost away from you, and a good protection ritual, such as the strong house cleansing in Part II, should prevent future attack. However, if you actually wronged the hungry ghost, such measures may send the ghost away once, but it will likely be back. In that case, the best thing would be to make any reparations possible and to make an offering at the person's grave and ask his or her forgiveness. If that fails, then a strong banishing ritual may be necessary.

Intelligent Ghost

VITAL STATISTICS

Danger Level: 1-6
Rarity: 5-6
Difficulty of Removal: 2-5
Where Found: Places where people spend significant amounts of time, particularly homes and places of work. Also found in places where strong emotions occurred.
Common Symptoms: Apparitions, phantom smells, disembodied voices, objects moving of their own accord, unexplained shadows, movement out of the corner of the eye, feelings of being watched.

LORE

This is the type of ghost most people think of when they think of hauntings. An intelligent ghost is a deceased person who, for whatever reason, does not move on to the next plane after death. It is commonly believed that this type of ghost remains on this plane due to having unfinished business on earth, or because it simply does not understand that it is no longer alive, but we cannot be sure. There is much speculation on why particular people become intelligent ghosts after death and others do not, but no one knows for certain.

An intelligent ghost can be distinguished from a residual haunting by its interactions with its surroundings. Unlike a residual haunting, intelligent ghosts will respond to people; they can respond to inquiries by speaking, moving objects, creating hot or cold spots, making sounds, or causing other unexplained phenomena, such as feelings of heaviness or of being watched. Some intelligent ghosts seem to have the ability to speak in voices that any person can hear, whereas others seem only to be able to communicate in a way that most people cannot hear with their ears, but that can be picked up by recording devices. This has led to the discovery of EVP, or Electronic Voice Phenomena, a recording of a disembodied voice that was not heard at the time it was recorded. There is much argument as to whether EVPs are the voices of ghosts or other metaphysical creatures, or if they are simply electronic artifacts.

An intelligent ghost can cause a very wide variety of phenomena. They can merely cause feelings of being watched and cold spots; they can appear as spectacular apparitions indistinguishable from the living; or they can cause objects to fly through the air. Intelligent ghosts seem to have varying levels of power, and thus varying ability to cause metaphysical phenomena. This is possibly dependent on the personality of the deceased, the age of the ghost, or natural phenomena at the location of the haunting, such as nearby running water, crystalline mineral deposits, storm energy, or ambient electromagnetic energy. For a more thorough discussion of power generated by natural phenomena see the entry on portals.

An intelligent ghost will usually haunt a location that had a particular significance to it in life, such as the place where it lived or worked, or a place that had strong emotional significance to it, such as the place where a traumatic event occurred. For example, a doctor may haunt the hospital she worked in, a man may haunt the house he lived in for 30 years, or a woman may haunt the location where she was murdered. In some rare instances, intelligent ghosts may haunt a person instead of a location. This usually happens when the ghost had a particular relationship to the person being haunted, such as that of spouse or child, or the ghost may need the person haunted to do something for it. In some cases, a ghost may haunt a person who wronged it out of revenge, but that is extremely rare.

Intelligent ghosts are as good or bad as the people they once were. The ghost of a very good person would do no harm. For example, the ghosts of deceased nurses often haunt the hospitals where they once worked and have been known to tuck people in at night or put extra blankets on the beds in winter. On the other hand, the ghost of a bad person would be as unpleasant as the person was in life and might delight in frightening people or even trying to harm them. That being said, most intelligent ghosts mean no harm. They are often just confused and frustrated.

In the rarest of cases, intelligent hauntings can become violent. It is possible, though incredibly unlikely, for a ghost to cause physical harm. A powerful ghost can throw objects, move furniture, and even bite, pinch, or scratch. In most cases, these extreme methods are only used to garner the attention of the living, but every once in a while a ghost is actively malevolent. In such cases, immediate banishing is often required. In such scenarios, strong banishings, such as the one presented in Part II, would be the most appropriate.

METHODS OF REMOVAL

Intelligent ghosts can be frightening, but rarely cause physical harm beyond a broken knick-knack or two. Accordingly, they can usually be left to their own devices and will move on when they feel ready. But if the people experiencing the haunting want it to stop now, there are three basic options:

1. Ask it to leave.
2. Aid it in moving on by helping it finish its business on earth.
3. Banish it.

It's always a good idea to firmly ask the ghost to leave before moving on to more intensive methods.

Quite often, an intelligent ghost feels the need to do something before it passes on. If you can learn to communicate with it, you may be able to help it accomplish its goal; once that goal is attained, the ghost will move on. The best way I have found to communicate with ghosts, if you do not have the innate talent, is to use divination, such as tarot cards or talking boards.

If you do find a way to communicate with the ghost, use common sense when speaking to it. Ghosts were people once and should always be treated with respect. Do ask them things like their name, when they lived, why they're still here, or if they need help. Don't call them derogatory names or badger them because they won't or can't make objects move; you wouldn't like it if they did that to you. Also, just like people, ghosts don't always tell the absolute truth, either because they don't know the whole truth or because they want to hide something. So when a ghost asks you to do something for them, use good judgment in deciding whether to do it or not.

If an intelligent ghost refuses to move on, you will have to perform a cleansing or even a banishing ritual (both of which are set out in detail in Part II).

Living Ghost

VITAL STATISTICS
Danger Level: 1
Rarity: 4
Difficulty of Removal: 1-3
Where Found: Anywhere.
Common Symptoms: Apparition of a living person.

LORE

A surprisingly common type of ghost is the living ghost. A living ghost is exactly what it sounds like: an apparition of a person who is still alive. This can happen when people leave their physical bodies and travel in their astral bodies. That astral body can sometimes be seen. (The astral body is the energetic part of a human being, which inhabits the physical body, but is distinct from it. Some believe the astral body is the soul or spirit of a person.) Essentially, a living ghost is the astral projection of a living person. This commonly occurs as the result of either bodily trauma or deliberate journeying. When such a body is seen, it is usually semi-transparent and may or may not be able to communicate normally.

One theory as to the cause of accidental astral projection is that intense physical trauma can "shock" the astral body out of the physical body. This is most common in cases of severe physical injury, such as a car accident, but can also occur when the body suffers long-term debilitation, as in the case of cancer treatments. The theory is that once the astral body is shocked out of the physical body by sudden injury, the injured person would consciously or unconsciously think of another person, and then the astral body would instantly go to that person. The astral body would return to the physical body either when the physical body was stabilized or when the mind was satisfied with whatever exchange it had with the witness. Similarly, the fatigue of longstanding illness can allow the astral body to separate from the physical and thus allow the astral body to wander.

When appearing to another person, the living ghost may or may not be aware that it is doing so. Some theorize that such an astral projection is little more than an emotional distress signal—a way of alerting a person's loved ones to his or her injury. Others believe that only extremely strong bonds between psychically gifted people allow for the appearance of a living ghost. It is true that living ghosts do not always appear when someone is gravely ill or injured, so it is possible that some kind of psychic gift is a precondition for their appearance. We may never know for certain.

Living ghosts are most often seen by the friends and relatives of an ill or injured person. However, it is also possible for total strangers to see a living ghost. If someone's astral body is shocked out of its physical body, it may simply hover near the physical body or wander aimlessly. In such cases, the living ghost could be seen by anyone nearby, particularly if they had the ability to see or sense energies on the astral level.

Of course, this doesn't apply when the appearance of the living ghost is the result of deliberate astral projection. Certain magickal practitioners or religious mystics actively engage in astral projection, most often seeking esoteric knowledge or some form of enlightenment. With practice, it is possible to cause the astral body to leave the physical body at will. Once freed of the physical, the astral body can travel around the world or even to other planes of existence. A skilled projector could potentially appear to anyone, regardless of the strength of their connection or the witness's ability to see the otherworldly. Fortunately, it is virtually unheard of for skilled projectors to use their abilities for anything other than personal growth.

METHODS OF REMOVAL

Most living ghosts appear only once and for a very short time. The average appearance lasts a few seconds, or at most a few minutes, and is usually for the purpose of alerting the loved one to the living ghost's situation or to say goodbye. Because living ghosts usually appear to loved ones, stopping the encounter is rarely a goal of the witness.

However, in incredibly rare cases, the witness may want the occurrence to stop. This situation would most likely occur in the case of a magickal practitioner purposefully appearing to someone repeatedly without his or her consent. Such cases are exceedingly rare and are generally easy to deal with: Astral travel is very difficult, requiring incredible concentration under even ideal circumstances; as such, proper shielding can usually stop these occurrences. Should shielding fail, doing a strong house cleansing and protection ritual would create wards sufficient to stop unwanted astral entities from entering the area. (For more information on shielding and house cleansing rituals, see Part II.)

Residual Ghost

VITAL STATISTICS

Danger Level: 1
Rarity: 3
Difficulty of Removal: 10
Where Found: Places of strong emotion or habit.
Common Symptoms: Apparitions that appear at the same place at the same time repeatedly, apparitions that do not interact with the real world, phantom sounds heard repeatedly at the same time.

LORE

A residual ghost (also called simply "a residual") is a ghost or group of ghosts that reenact some event from the past—ghostly soldiers fighting the Battle of Gettysburg over and over again, or the ghost of a woman that walks down the same hallway each night, for example. These ghosts do not interact with the mundane world; they simply repeat something they once did. If a residual ghost walks a particular path each night, and then a wall is put up in its path, it would walk straight through the wall as if it did not exist. This kind of ghost is completely benign; it cannot do harm. In fact, it cannot interact with the physical world at all.

Residuals can appear as faint glowing lights, semi-transparent figures, or fully formed apparitions that are almost indistinguishable from the living. Residuals can be differentiated from other types of ghosts in that they always do the exact same thing. Usually, residuals can be seen repeating their movements at regular intervals: every night at midnight, once a month, every July 13th, and so on. If you speak to a residual or move into its path it will ignore you; it does not even know you are there.

Though people are the most common subjects, they are not the only things that can appear as residual ghosts. Sometimes inanimate objects appear as residual ghosts. The most common type of inanimate object seen as a residual ghost is transportation vehicles. There are numerous accounts of people seeing phantom vehicles or hearing the sound of a train on an unused bit of track. For example, many witnesses have reported seeing a fleet of WWII era fighter planes throughout the years off the coast of Florida that were lost many years ago. Similarly, animals can also appear as residual ghosts. This is most common in the case of family pets that are seen sleeping in their customary spots or eating out of their food bowls in the time after their deaths. For whatever reason, animal residuals do not tend to last as long as other types of residual ghosts, often only being seen within a month or so of their passing.

There are several theories as to what causes residual hauntings. A popular one is that what we see is the imprint of an act of great emotional significance on the place where it happened. For example, one might see a figure reenacting its death or some other traumatic event. Another theory is that repetition of actions, such as going up a staircase, walking down a hallway, or always sitting in a particular chair, causes so much energy to be given off in a particular pattern that it sinks into the location itself and can be seen by those sensitive to such energies. This would explain seeing the ghost of one's grandfather sitting in his favorite chair.

Yet another popular theory is that residual hauntings are caused, in part, by high concentrations of minerals such as quartz or limestone that can absorb and store strong energies. The idea is that strong emotions throw off energy, which is absorbed by the minerals and then released at periodic intervals through an as-yet-unknown natural process.

METHODS OF REMOVAL

Because echoes do not do any harm, they can usually be left alone; in time, they will sometimes fade away on their own. Other times, because they have been repeating their actions for so long and their energy is do deeply imprinted on their surroundings, they can be almost impossible to get rid of. Possible reasons for wanting to get rid of an echo would be if the image was gruesome or unpleasant (such as a soldier missing half his limbs), or perhaps if it was distracting (you'd hardly want to take a test with the image of ghostly children dancing on your desk). If you feel you must remove an echo the best thing to do is a strong magical cleansing of the area, such as the strong house cleansing or strong banishing presented in Part II. Unfortunately, even the strongest of cleansings is unlikely to wash away 50 years of repeated action, and thus is unlikely to be successful the first time around. You may have to repeat such rituals on a regular basis—possibly for years—before you are successful.

Revenant

VITAL STATISTICS
Danger Level: 7-9
Rarity: 9
Difficulty of Removal: 8-9
Where Found: Near desecrated graves, crossroads, places where the revenant once lived.
Common Symptoms: Shambling corpse rising from the grave, often subsequently attacking the living. They are unsubtle.

LORE

Though the term *revenant* can be used to refer to any kind of undead creature, such as vampires and ghosts, in this guide, the term shall specifically refer to any corpse that rises physically from the grave. Stories of revenants exist in almost every culture in the world; for example, the Draugr, Haugbui, Oupire, Pisacha, Sundal Bolong, and, of course, the zombie. Revenants can vary widely in their appearance; some are indistinguishable from living humans, but far more of them look like decaying corpses, with blue or black skin, long fingernails, and obvious rot.

The reasons revenants rise from the grave varies from culture to culture. In some lore only evildoers rise as revenants, such as with the traditional English Revenant. In such cases, the spirit of the deceased is unable to move on, and is essentially trapped in its decaying corpse. This makes an already evil person even angrier and more violent than in life, and thus more likely to do evil wherever it can. For example, the Draugr of Viking lore are believed to be created when a very active and malevolent person dies. Due to their violent personalities and high energy, these people do not lie quietly upon death and will rise and continue the kinds of activities they pursued in life, such as pillaging the countryside.

In other lore revenants are created when people are improperly buried or their graves are desecrated. Such desecration allows evil spirits to inhabit the corpse, which is then used to commit violence on all around it. These revenants often evince powers of the supernatural beings that inhabit them, such as the ability to control mists or the weather. Revenants that rise from desecrated graves are more likely to be vampiric than other revenants.

The most famous kind of walking dead is, without question, the zombie. According to popular superstition, evil Voodoo practitioners, called Bokors, can use their magickal powers to literally raise the dead from their graves and enslave the raised zombies to their will. Anthropologists believe that this lore originated in Haiti when certain Bokors allegedly poisoned people with a toxin that mimics death, called tetrodotoxin. They then buried the poisoned people alive, and then "resurrected" them. The combination of the poison and the shock and oxygen deprivation of burial would damage the brains of the victims in such a way that they lost their personalities and were extremely pliable, following any orders given them. Such people are, of course, not revenants, but victims of a terrible crime. It is doubtful, though not patently impossible, that a physical manifestation of the popular idea of an undead zombie actually exists.

METHODS OF REMOVAL

All the lore agrees that revenants are thoroughly evil and very difficult to kill. The problem is that revenants are already dead, so they can take quite a bit of damage before they are stopped. Some revenants, like the Pisacha of India, can be killed by a sword through the heart, or beheading. Other revenants, like the Draugr, are virtually invincible. The best way to stop a rampaging revenant is to utterly destroy its body, either through fire, dismemberment, or incredible firepower.

Traditional lore has many suggestions for how to deal with revenants. Some lore suggests that they can be repelled by things like garlic and holy or blessed items. This holds true most strongly for revenants that are supernatural beings inhabiting human corpses, and less so against reanimated evildoers—unless the blessed object is of their faith. Slavic lore also suggests that, like the vampire, a revenant's resting place can be approached safely during the day, and the revenant can then be staked through the heart. This is not done to destroy the revenant, but to pin it to the ground so that it cannot rise. This may or may not work; thorough dismemberment is a surer way to prevent a revenant from rising again.

Shadow People

VITAL STATISTICS

Danger Level: 2

Rarity: 3

Difficulty of Removal: 2-5

Where Found: Older buildings.

Common Symptoms: Seeing a shadowy figure out of the corner of eye; a short, shadowy figure appearing in photos or video; feeling of being watched.

Dead and Undead

LORE

Shadow people are shadowy humanoid figures that are 3 to 4 feet tall and are seen in older buildings and homes. Such figures are usually seen out of the corner of the eye, often when they are least expected, rather than head-on. Although such phenomena has been relatively common for many years, shadow people were thought to be just another form of haunting by ghosts. But in recent times, since the use of still and video cameras become ubiquitous in ghost hunting, people have begun to theorize that shadow people may not be ghosts at all. Instead, they may be a metaphysical creature completely separate from ghosts. Shadow people do not appear to be malevolent; there are no reported incidents of people being harmed by them; they're just a little frightening.

Shadow people appear exactly the way one might imagine: as dark, shadowy human figures. Often they appear as little more than human-shaped black masses, but they are sometimes more clearly defined humanoid bodies with distinctive heads, arms, and legs. It is also not uncommon for witnesses to report them as wearing hats or hoods. However, reports of shadow people appearing to wear particular kinds of clothing are rather suspect. Shadow people often lack definition in their form, and that lack of definition could be interpreted by the witness as loose clothing, particularly hoods. The figures may appear wispy and intangible or quite solid; there seems to be no explanation as to why some shadow people are more or less well defined than others. It is also common for them to appear on film or video footage when they were not physically seen at the time of recording. When they are seen or their images captured, they often appear to be moving away from the observer, as if they do not want to be seen.

Those who are sensitive to metaphysical energy may be able to sense the presence of shadow people. When one examines an empty room with one's metaphysical senses, the energy should feel even and undisturbed, like the surface of a calm pond. When there is something in a room that cannot be seen with the eyes, one's metaphysical senses may pick up a feeling of disturbance, heaviness, or foreign energy where that creature stands—like seeing the ripples of water where it meets a rock. This feeling of disturbance or presence alerts the sensitive to the presence of something unseen, but unless the sensitive knows what the energy of different creatures "feels" like, he or she will probably not be able to tell what that presence is.

The presence of shadow people can be very difficult to distinguish from the presence of other metaphysical creatures. Many creatures can appear as shadowy figures seen out of the corner of the eye, such as ghosts, pixies, imps, and goblins. The main distinction between shadow people and other creatures (other than ghosts) is that they will usually appear humanoid. The best way to determine the difference between shadow people and ghosts is to look at their behavior. Residual ghosts will perform the same action over and over again, whereas shadow people do not. Intelligent ghosts will often try to communicate with the living by causing haunting phenomena; shadow people do not seem interested in doing so.

The only evidence of the presence of shadow people is sightings of them, the feeling of being watched, and the feeling of a foreign presence in an otherwise empty space. If those symptoms are the *only* things happening, then you may be dealing with shadow people. If there are any other symptoms present, you should look elsewhere for their source.

No one knows what shadow people really are; they may be ghosts, faeries, or something altogether different. The fact that they often appear in photos and videos when they were not physically seen at the time argues for them being something that does not dwell entirely on this plane of existence. Unfortunately, that applies to just about every creature in this book, so this information tells us very little about their nature. It's also possible that shadow people are not a separate type of creature at all, but are instead a form taken by several different creatures. We may never know the truth.

METHODS OF REMOVAL

As they are harmless, there's really no reason to remove shadow people from a building unless the occupants are very uncomfortable with it. In that case, have the occupants of the building firmly ask the shadow people to leave, and explain why. In most cases, that will be the end of things. If that fails, then a basic cleansing ritual, such as the simple house cleansing in Part II, should suffice.

– 6 –

Malignant Magick

As anyone who has lived in the world knows, not all people are good. Most people muddle along and live their lives as best as they can, but some people feel the need to take short-cuts to get what they want and don't care who gets hurt in the process—magickal practitioners are no different. Most people who use magick do so out of a desire to do good, but it isn't always done wisely. Some few practitioners even use magick for greed, revenge, and just plain malevolence. When magick is done improperly or with baneful intent, you get malignant magick. Some of the following entries, such as the curse and the thoughtform, are in this section for obvious reasons—they are forms of magick that can be used to do great harm. The inclusion of two other entries, for Elementals and shape-shifters, is less obvious. Those entries are listed in this section because they are rarely a problem when malignant magick is not involved. For example, Elementals are creatures of nature that normally have little to no interaction with people; they will (usually) only become a threat when magickally interfered with. So whether they be creatures or forms of magick themselves, all the entries in this section are only a danger when malignant magick is involved.

127

Curse

VITAL STATISTICS

Danger Level: 1-8

Rarity: 7 (The rarity of this malignant magick is based on curses that are actually dangerous or strong enough for the cursee to notice.)

Difficulty of Removal: 1-8 (The danger level and difficulty of removal depend entirely on the severity of the curse and the force of the intent behind it. For example, an accidental curse born from annoyance would be less dangerous and easier to deal with than a deliberate curse set by a skilled magickal practitioner.)

Where Found: Everywhere.

Common Symptoms: Uncommon bad luck, ill health, nightmares, befuddlement, lack of energy, a feeling of oppression, and more.

LORE

A curse, or hex, is malignant magick designed to do harm to its target. It can be as simple as swearing at a driver who cuts off the curser in traffic, or as complicated as a ritual by an angry magickal practitioner. Effectively, most curses are balls of negative energy that are hurled at the target. This negative energy then surrounds the target, influencing his or her energy and causing all manner of trouble. A curse can do anything from make someone stub a toe to causing a person to have a major car accident.

Folklore is full of stories about magickal practitioners gone wrong and the evil curses they perpetrate. Whether it's a jealous sorceress turning her rival into a pig or a greedy warlock teleporting his neighbor's gold into his own coffers, stories intimate that magickal practitioners can do some very impressive things. Whereas this makes for an exciting story, real curses are not so fantastical. A real curse is far more likely to undermine a rival's confidence or make a business competitor forget what he was going to say. Real magick is subtle rather than flashy.

The most common symptoms that can indicate the presence of a curse are uncommon bad luck and lingering ill health. As noted, a curse is made from energy, and thus can most easily influence the *energy* of another, rather than the physical. Negative energy settling in the body can affect one's moods and can easily make one lose concentration. This can result in what seems like a run of bad luck, because it "puts you off your game," so to speak. Negative energy makes it very difficult for our minds and bodies to perform at their best. For this same reason, it can create ill health. Our health is directly linked to our energy levels. Negative energy saps vitality and can leave the body more vulnerable, making it prone to illness. However, this physical effect is less common than the mental feeling of being "off."

To the psychically gifted, there is an even easier way to identify the presence of a curse. One who has the ability to sense magickal energies may be able to sense it. When someone has been cursed, he or she may emit a feeling of oppression or a feeling of being bound in some way. Some curses can also be seen in the aura of the afflicted. (Very simply, an aura is a person's energy field. It is often seen as a halo of colored light emanating from the body about six inches and fading off into the distance.) For someone with the ability to see auras, a curse may look like dark threads wrapped around the victim, or dark goo surrounding or splattered about the victim's aura. The ability to see or feel magickal energies can be natural talent, or it can be something learned through practice. (However, such instruction is beyond the scope of this guide.)

True curses and psychic attacks are extremely rare. But if someone truly believes himself to be under attack or cursed, he can effectively curse himself. Once a person believes she is cursed, she will start to see every minor misfortune in her life as part of the "curse"—if she misses a green light, it was part of the curse; if she fails to get promoted, it was part of the curse; if she stains her favorite shirt, you guessed it, part of the curse. This creates a downward spiral of negativity that can potentially affect the person's life as much as any malevolent magick.

Methods of Removal

The best way to deal with a curse or supposed curse is to perform a hex-breaking ritual (presented in Part II). Hex-breaking rituals are appropriate whenever a person believes him- or herself to be under psychic attack from another person, or if they believe themselves to be "cursed," regardless of whether he or she really is or not. A hex-breaking is essentially a very powerful personal cleansing ritual, and it works just as well on self-generated negative energy as it does on that from outside sources.

You may occasionally run into a person who firmly believes he's cursed, and further, he's convinced that he knows exactly who's cursing him. Such a person may try to get you to do a hex-breaking that will send the negative energy back to whomever it is he believes has cursed him. Don't do it. It's likely that this person has inadvertently caused his own suffering and the other person is largely innocent. To send a hex back to someone who may or may not have actually caused the hex in the first place is an enormous breach of ethics. In such a case, you should gently but firmly explain that a hex-breaking is about clearing the hexee of negative energy and negative outside influences, not about punishing the hexer.

Elemental

VITAL STATISTICS
Danger Level: 7
Rarity: 8
Difficulty of Removal: 8
Where Found: Everywhere, but more common in the wild or where uncontrolled magick has been practiced.
Common Symptoms: Imbalance in nature, out-of-place natural phenomena (like hail on a cloudless day), the physical appearance of strange Elemental creatures.

Malignant Magick

LORE

An Elemental is a physically embodied nature spirit, representative of one of the four elements: earth, air, fire, and water. In folklore, specific creatures are identified with each element: gnomes with earth, sylphs with air, salamanders with fire, and undines with water. These are generally friendly spirits with which people with metaphysical sensitivity can learn to communicate. Such communication is usually accomplished either through telepathy or a divination tool such as a pendulum or tarot cards. Friendly Elementals live wherever their element is strongest; you can find earth Elementals in caves and on mountains, air Elementals on windswept cliffs and on top of tall buildings, fire Elementals in volcanoes and actual fires, and water Elementals in rivers, springs, and oceans. Naturally occurring Elementals are both rare and shy, living only in the most pristine and unspoiled environments. As a result, humans very rarely come in contact with them. People are much more likely to encounter summoned Elementals—elemental spirits summoned by magickal practitioners to aid them in their work.

When most magickal practitioners work with Elementals, it is for benign purposes and usually on the astral plane—a non-corporeal magickal dimension. Elementals can teach magickal practitioners about the nature of the element and how to work with it. This teaching is usually accomplished through meditation and divination with non-corporeal Elementals that leave the area once they've finished speaking to the practitioner. However, in some exceptionally rare cases, the Elemental may manifest physically. This happens when the practitioner is very strong, the location of the magickal working has its own energy that is aligned with the element being worked with, or more often a combination of the two. Even such rare cases would not normally be dangerous. The problem is when the practitioner is not using his or her power for good or the manifested Elemental is improperly dismissed when the working is over.

Whenever a magickal practitioner chooses to work with an outside entity, he or she must summon the entity, do his or her magickal working, and then dismiss the entity. Dismissing an entity after a working is very important because most summoned entities do not belong in this plane and should not be here for long periods of time. Imagine having to travel a long distance because a friend needs your help, and your friend pays your travel expenses. You get there, you help your friend, and when you're done the friend never tells you that you can leave or gets you a return ticket home—now you're stuck far from home with someone whom you may feel has taken advantage of you. Now imagine that you're that annoyed and a very powerful magickal entity. See how that could cause problems?

A strong enough unethical practitioner could potentially summon an Elemental and use it to do harm. As are all natural forces, Elementals are morally neutral—their actions can have beneficial or baneful effects depending entirely on how they are directed. Elementals are also mentally simple creatures; they know their element and they know what their summoner tells them. This lack of sophistication means that they cannot discern for themselves whether they should do what their summoner tells them; they just do it. Elementals have all the power of their element; for example, earth Elementals are strong, air Elementals are cunning, fire Elementals are wild, and water Elementals are implacable. (Note that air Elementals, though cunning, are still simple-minded in that they cannot think outside the scope of whatever task has been set before them. However, they can display great cunning in accomplishing that task.) Elementals can wreak just about any kind of havoc you can imagine and can even cause natural disasters. An Elemental is a terrible weapon to have in the wrong hands.

The danger with improperly dismissed Elementals is that they are not meant to exist on this plane for more than a short time. Summoned Elementals are manifestations of their element and the will of the summoner, and are meant to fade back into their element when the practitioner is done with them. When not allowed to do so, the Elemental will often get quite angry and may even go slightly mad. No one wants a creature with that kind of power to go mad. In such an unsettled and unnatural state, Elementals will lash out uncontrollably in any way they know how in an attempt to find a way back to their natural state.

Malignant Magick

METHODS OF REMOVAL

Dealing with an Elemental requires a fair amount of magickal experience. If you are not an experienced practitioner you should seek aid from one.

For the experienced practitioner: In order to dispel an Elemental you did not summon, you must first take control of it (to have the kind of control a summoner would have), and then properly dismiss it. The following ritual (included here as opposed to Part II because it is specific to Elementals only) should work.

To Dispel an Errant Elemental

You must first know what element you're dealing with, and then gather icons of that element: rocks and dirt for earth, feathers and incense for air, candles and a blade for fire, a cup of water and some shells for water. Also gather whatever ritual accoutrement you feel necessary (for example, if you always cast with a wand, you should use it here).

- ◎ *Gird yourself with whatever method of magickal protection you prefer. For example, anoint yourself with protective oils, invoke protective spirits or deities, and/or carry protective amulets.*

- ◎ *Go to the physical location where the Elemental lives or has been spotted. Find a clear spot with plenty of room in front of you.*

- ◎ *Summon your will. If you don't know that you have the power to command it, the Elemental won't take you seriously.*

- ◎ *Say:*

Elemental of [element]. You do not belong here. Show yourself!

With all the force of your will, visualize the Elemental appearing before you. After a few moments, it should. If it doesn't, repeat the invocation up to three times. If it still doesn't show, it's either gone or not going to respond to you, in which case you'll need to find help.

🜨 *Once the Elemental appears, envision your will forming a transparent sphere around it. Envision the sphere tightening around it. As it pulls in tight to the Elemental's surface, say:*

Creature of [element], I bind you to my will.

🜨 *As you say the following, envision the Elemental losing cohesion and slowly retreating back to its element (a pile of dirt, a breeze, or the like):*

Creature of [element], you do not belong here. Return to [element]. Your work is finished here; it is time to return from whence you came. Rest. I dispel you, creature of [element]. Be no more.

At this point, the Elemental should have faded to nothing.

Doppelgänger

VITAL STATISTICS

Danger Level: 3-5

Rarity: 7

Difficulty of Removal: 7

Where Found: Near people who have been through some sort of mental trauma.

Common Symptoms: Hearing a voice that no one else can hear, seeing a person or shadow constantly out of the corner of the eye, feeling stalked.

Malignant Magick

LORE

The doppelgänger, also called a fetch, is essentially the shadow side of a human being. Under normal circumstances, this shadow self is contained within the psyche and is no more dangerous than the ever-present darker side of any person. However, through psychic calamity, such as a malevolent spell or severe mental trauma, the doppelgänger can gain independence from the psyche, either manifesting as a separate personality or even a physical being (though that is incredibly rare.) When a person with a strong shadow side goes through intense mental stress, it is possible for that shadow side, comprising all of a person's darker impulses and thoughts, to gather and concentrate until it coalesces into a separate and independent mind. It is important to note that having a strong shadow side is by no means an indication that someone is a bad person. Often it indicates quite the contrary. A strong, separate shadow self usually means that the person simply has difficulty accepting his or her darker thoughts and impulses, and, unfortunately, this lack of acceptance can give dark thoughts more strength, rather than less. But the less someone's darker thoughts are a part of his or her normal personality, the more likely they are to shear off into a separate mind during trauma. Unfortunately, once separated from their hosts, doppelgängers seem to become not only the embodiment of their host's basest thoughts, but also a magnification of them—with far darker and more dangerous impulses than the hosts ever had. Thankfully, doppelgängers have no real power except that of suggestion and a deep knowledge of their hosts that gives them a psychological edge.

Once a doppelgänger has developed into an independent personality, it is usually only seen or heard by the individual from whom it is derived. Because the doppelgänger was once part of the host personality, that person will always have a sort of harmony with it, like a pair of radios tuned to the same frequency. This allows the host and the doppelgänger to see and communicate with one another, even when other people are unaware of the doppelgänger's presence. In such cases, the doppelgänger whispers into the mind of its host, tempting him or her to do terrible things that are far outside his or her natural character—essentially acting as the proverbial "shoulder devil." However, in some cases, the doppelgänger is benign and actually offers advice and insight to its host. This rare occurrence tends to happen when the host has a very passive personality; the doppelgänger will berate the milquetoast and force him to stand up for himself. Such benevolent cases are virtually unheard of today, with the more malevolent "advice" being the norm.

In other cases, the doppelgänger can actually take over the body of its host and do with it what it will, effectively possessing the host. (For more detailed information see the entry on possession.) The most famous account of such a case is in Robert Louis Stevenson's tale *Dr. Jekyll and Mr. Hyde*, in which the mild-mannered Doctor Jekyll takes a potion that unleashes his doppelgänger, Mr. Hyde, and allows him to take over the doctor's body for a short period of time. While in possession of the doctor's body, Mr. Hyde acts only on his basest impulses and perpetrates terrible crimes. Though fictional, this tale does show the absolute worst-case scenario for possession by a doppelgänger. In reality, a doppelgänger is much more likely to have verbal or physical altercations with its host's enemies and to be brutally honest with its host's friends and family, likely saying and doing things that will irrevocably alter relationships. Thankfully, such possession is much rarer than simply having a doppelgänger urging its host to act on its baser impulses.

In the very rarest of cases, a doppelgänger may gain an independent body. Such a body is usually only astral and lacks real physical substance. As mentioned previously, doppelgängers and their hosts have a sort of harmony that will allow a prior host to see a separated doppelgänger's astral body even when others cannot. That body may appear as a full-bodied apparition or no more than an insubstantial shadow. A separated doppelgänger is stronger and has more metaphysical energy than one that is still attached to its host, making a separated doppelgänger easier for the metaphysically sensitive to see. Such people might see the doppelgänger in the same way that its prior host would, or may simply sense a malevolent presence or even a cold spot where the doppelgänger stands. Though it is theoretically possible (because nothing is truly impossible), there are no records or folklore of a doppelgänger ever growing so powerful that it gains its own independent physical body.

METHODS OF REMOVAL

The most difficult part of dealing with a doppelgänger is identifying it. The presence of a doppelgänger is virtually indistinguishable from several serious mental illnesses, and can actually appear in conjunction with or even cause them. Conditions such as schizophrenia and dissociative identity disorder can have identical symptoms as the presence of a doppelgänger. Further complicating matters is the fact that a doppelgänger can drive its host insane, causing such mental illnesses.

These mental conditions are serious and require professional help. In such circumstances, it is best to first seek professional help from a psychologist or psychiatrist before attempting any magickal remedies. If at all possible, try to find a mental health professional that is "magick positive," or at least does not view all belief in the metaphysical as a symptom of mental illness—it will make your life easier. Then, with the permission of the professional, do a magickal cleansing and protection ritual along the lines of a hex-breaking for the affected person. The hex-breaking rituals presented in Part II should be effective in such situations; use the hex-breaking of a strength commensurate with the severity of the symptoms the doppelgänger has created. Even if the affected person does not actually have a doppelgänger, these cleansings are unlikely to do further harm and can be quite effective psychosomatically, even when their magick is unnecessary. Of course, if there is a doppelgänger present, such rituals will do a world of good.

Portal

VITAL STATISTICS

Danger Level: 2-7

Rarity: 4

Difficulty of Removal: 3-7 (The danger level and difficulty of removal depend on how the portal was formed and where it leads.)

Where Found: Can be anywhere, but most common in places where large amounts of energy (positive or negative-have been released) and places where magick has gone wrong.

Common Symptoms: Presence of many metaphysical creatures that seem to originate from one spot, a feeling of being pulled to a particular spot, magick being particularly potent in one spot, time seeming to pass differently in a particular place.

LORE

Portals are places where the boundary between this world and another are so thin that energy and creatures can pass through. There are many names for portals, including vortices, power spots, thinnies, and holes. Most people do encounter a portal or two during their lives, but very few recognize them for what they are. Portals can be of any size or shape, from a dime to a football field. Their size and shape can be fixed, like a doorway, or it can be fluid, changing shape and size according to energy fluctuations, time of year, or other unknown factors.

The presence of a portal can be detected in a number of ways, the most obvious of which is to actually see something move in or out of it, but such sightings are rare. More likely, people will report ongoing strangeness in a particular area. People may notice that, in a particular area, time can seem to run more quickly or slowly than normal, magick can be extremely potent, disembodied voices can be heard whispering, unseen creatures can be felt scurrying near your feet, or visions can be had. People may also report feeling odd physical sensations near a portal, such as dizziness, headaches, the feeling of extra energy running through the body, or a prickling sensation at the base of the spine, neck, or in the palms of the hands. Unfortunately, such phenomena are not unique to the presence of a portal.

The presence of a portal can be similar to a haunting, and the difference can be difficult to determine. The main difference is in the localization of phenomena. In a haunting, paranormal phenomena are often reported in specific places or at specific times. If the phenomena occur at the same time and place repeatedly, they are likely the result of a haunting. The localization of phenomena in fairly large areas, such as an entire house or forest, also indicates a haunting rather than a portal. However, if the phenomena become more and more concentrated as you approach a particular location, then a portal is likely the cause. To make matters more confusing, the presence of a portal can *cause* a haunting because the portal may draw ghosts or other unseen creatures to a particular location. In such cases, only someone with the ability to sense unseen energies will be able to determine whether a portal is present. For such people, portals often feel like a whirlpool, either sucking in or spitting out energy, and the portal's energy will stand out very distinctly from the energy around it. (Thankfully for those without such extrasensory perceptions, making a certain distinction between hauntings and portals is often unnecessary because the methods of removal are largely the same.)

Portals are gateways. As such, they are not intrinsically good or bad, but what comes through them may be. Depending on the size and strength of a portal, it may allow for communication between worlds, the transfer of energies, or astral and even physical movement between worlds. The nature of a portal depends largely on the kind of energy that created it. Portals created purely by natural energies tend to be quite neutral, sometimes allowing positive things to pass and other times allowing negative things to pass. Portals created by magickal energies or the sudden release of large amounts of emotional energy tend to connect to places that correspond with the positivity or negativity that created them. Portals created by long use of benevolent magick tend to connect to places inhabited by beneficial energies, whereas those created by negative energies often connect to places of great negativity, inhabited by very unpleasant things.

Small portals can be quite useful for magickal practitioners, as they make working with otherworldly powers easier. However, one must be cautious when working with portals. It is very difficult to know what's on the other side of a portal, making working with them rather risky. As not all metaphysical beings tell the truth, you can never be absolutely certain about what you're working with. Further, the continued transfer of magickal energies through a portal can essentially "feed" the portal, making it larger and more powerful, or unstable, causing it to vary in its size and strength, or even change the location to which it leads.

Portals are created when energy is concentrated, either in large amounts at one time or in smaller amounts throughout a long period of time, to the point at which it bleeds through from this world into another. Such concentrations can occur in a number of ways. Most portals are created naturally by topographical features and latent energies in the earth. Every landscape on earth contains natural energy. Such energy can be seen in the growth of plants, the shifting winds, the push of flowing lava, ocean currents, and many other things. Where these energies come together or are concentrated, portals can appear. For example, a portal may appear in a place where the bedrock has large deposits of quartz crystal and is crossed by running water. The running water generates continuous energy and the quartz crystals can act as batteries, holding and concentrating the natural energy. These energies can build up until they actually penetrate into other planes of existence, creating a portal.

Similarly, the buildup of magickal energy over time, or the release of very large amounts of it, can create a portal. It is not uncommon for magickal practitioners to perform their magick in one particular place, often a space that is set apart for this purpose alone. In time, these magickal energies will sink into the location itself, just as dust settles on a doormat every time you cross the threshold. As long as the practitioner occasionally cleanses his or her workspace (think of shaking the aforementioned doormat), this buildup of energies presents no threat. However, some practitioners are less diligent, and others let such energies build up on purpose. The problem arises when the practitioner then leaves his or her working space and someone else comes to occupy it.

The release of large amounts of energy, whether mundane or magickal, at one time can also create a portal. A large release of energy into any environment is traumatic for that environment. Imagine digging a hole in a garden and then filling it with water. If you fill it slowly, drop by drop, the ground will absorb the water and the hole will never overflow. However, if you fill it too quickly, the ground won't have time to absorb all the excess water and the hole will overflow. Similarly, large amounts of energy can overwhelm an environment's ability to contain it. The overflow, whether of traumatic emotions or deliberate magick, has to go somewhere, and that is often accomplished by punching a hole into another realm. For energy released all at once, it seems that negative energy is more likely to create a portal. Why this should be is unknown; perhaps the earth simply has more trouble absorbing negative energies.

Portals become a problem when they grow too large, allowing too much movement between worlds, or if they lead to unpleasant places. Small, weak portals do not allow much to move through them, minimizing any danger around them—a haunting voice or an imp or two are of little consequence. Large, strong portals, on the other hand, can allow many things to pass through them. As this guide attests, not all creatures from other planes are pleasant. Just because something is otherworldly does not mean that it wants to help us attain a higher state of being, and a portal into a demonic plane could allow truly horrible creatures into our world.

METHODS OF REMOVAL

Most portals do not require our interference; it is only those that allow negative energy to pass from another world into ours that must be dealt with. Naturally occurring portals rarely grow large enough or connect to negative enough places to be a problem. This is fortunate, because the only reliable way to close them is to alter the natural features that created them in the first place—no easy feat, and probably illegal if you don't own the land. However, if the portal is small enough, you may be able to ground the energy coming out of it by burying a small hematite, black tourmaline, or other grounding stone at the rim of the portal. Portals created by negative energy or magick are more likely to be a problem.

To close a portal created by negative energy or magick, you will have to neutralize that negative force. For a small portal, the strewing of salt and/or blessed water can be sufficient to dispel the negative energies, as can simple cleansings. The release of large amounts of positive energy, such as that given off by a lively party or other joyful activities, can also neutralize a negative portal, depending on its strength. For a large portal, this is most easily done by clergy who have had much practice in giving blessings. Strong religious blessings given by those who truly believe will almost always neutralize the negative energy that created the portal, closing it permanently. If you do not have access to an understanding clergy-person, a strong cleansing ritual should do the trick. (Both basic and strong house-cleansing rituals are described step by step in Part II.)

Possession

VITAL STATISTICS
Danger Level: 5-9
Rarity: 8
Difficulty of Removal: 7-9 (The danger level and difficulty of removal depend on the entity doing the possessing and the willpower of the person being possessed.)
Where Found: Everywhere.
Common Symptoms: Extreme shift in personality, wasting illness, speaking in tongues, feeling of not being alone in one's mind, irrepressible urges, acting out of character and not knowing why.

LORE

Possession is one of the rarest and most frightening magickal maladies one can encounter. It occurs when some kind of entity comes into a person's body and tries to take it over. The possessing entity can force the person being possessed to do things he or she would not normally do or are against his or her character. To the outsider, it can seem as though the person being possessed is losing his or her mind. To the more perceptive, it may seem as though someone else is looking out from the possessed person's eyes. Possession can last anywhere from just a few moments to days, weeks, months, and possibly longer. Possession has been known to happen with doppelgängers, some kinds of faeries, and demons.

In most cases when possession is attempted by an outside entity, the strength of the host's (the person being taken over) personality will keep possession from actually occurring. However, things like illness, feeble-mindedness, or curses can weaken a person to the point that he or she is more vulnerable to outside possession. The strength of the mind is as important for preventing possession as a strong immune system is for preventing disease. The most important mental factors in preventing possession are sense of self and identity, and willpower. A strong sense of self—knowing who and what we are—can create a mental barrier against anything that would alter the self, be it unkind words from a friend or an outside entity seeking to invade. That strong sense of self would also notice anything attempting to alter or control the self and try to force it out. The strength of one's willpower would determine just how hard the mind would fight against an invader. People who are secure in who and what they are would be far less vulnerable to possession than those who are unsure of themselves and struggling to find their identity. However, that is not to say that the insecure are necessarily vulnerable to possession, because even they can have wills of iron.

Though movies such as *The Exorcist* and *The Exorcism of Emily Rose* would have us believe that possession is violent, dangerous, and terribly obvious, that is not always the case. Possession most often manifests as a sudden and dramatic shift in a person's personality evinced by acting out of character, speaking with knowledge he or she should not have, a change in mannerisms, and even a change in the sound of his or her voice. For example, a normally cheerful person may suddenly become sullen and angry, or a person who was previously left-handed may suddenly become right-handed.

Possession can manifest to the host as hearing voices, a feeling of oppression, the feeling of not being alone in one's mind, and the loss of time—not knowing where one was or what one was doing for a time. In the rarest of cases things such as speaking in tongues, violent outbursts, or spectacular psychic ability—such as clairvoyance or psychokinesis—may occur. In most cases, possession is little more than an overzealous haunting by a mischievous spirit that lasts for a few moments before the possessee's will pushes out the invading entity, like white blood cells eliminating germs. In these cases, little harm and much embarrassment is the result. In the rarest of cases, people can harm themselves and others, or even go mad.

METHODS OF REMOVAL

One of the greatest difficulties in dealing with possession is diagnosis. From the outside, possession can look like a number of mental illnesses, such as schizophrenia or multiple personality disorder. These are serious conditions that require professional care. Consequently, if you think there is even the slightest possibility that they might be present, you should seek the aid of a mental health professional.

Another difficulty in diagnosis is that people change; sometimes dramatically. If your child suddenly shifts personality and begins behaving inappropriately, chances are good that he or she has hit puberty—not that he or she is possessed. If a 50-year-old man suddenly quits his job, divorces his wife, and buys a sports car, you're probably dealing with nothing more than a mid-life crisis. Possession is incredibly rare, so regardless of the symptoms, chances are very good that whatever you're dealing with is something more mundane.

The level of difficulty in dealing with possession, when it happens, depends entirely on the strength of the being doing the possessing. As such, the first order of business is to find out what the possessor is. Depending on the violence of the possession, you may be able to simply ask the possessor what it is; often it will tell you. If the possessor will not identify itself, you will have to look for other symptoms that might identify it and compare them with the creatures in this guide. If that fails, your only real option is to find someone skilled at identifying such creatures and asking them for help.

Once you've identified the possessor, you can follow the methods of removal outlined in its entry (such as the demon and the doppelgänger) to remove it. If the possessor is not particularly strong, then the Elemental hex-breaking in Part II may be helpful.

Shape-Shifter

VITAL STATISTICS

Danger Level: 1-7

Rarity: 5-9

Difficulty of Removal: 1-8

Where Found: Everywhere.

Common Symptoms: Most common shape-shifters have no overt symptoms. Rarely: disappearances during full moon, sensitivity to silver, disappearance or death of small animals.

LORE

Almost every culture on earth has stories of shape-shifters, also called theriomorphs. The shape-shifters in these stories include but are not limited to: werewolves, Jaguar Shaman, Kitsune, Tengu, Naga, Kelpies, were-hyenas, Selkies, Nagual, Skin-Walkers, Anjing Ajak, Asuang, Berserkers, Bouda, Farkaskoldus, Hamrammr, Ilimu, Loup-Garou, Manananggal, and Runaturunco. Shape-shifting myths are extremely common. In lore, shape-shifting can be done voluntarily or involuntarily: A shape-shifter may consciously will himself to shift at particular times, or may be forced to change under particular conditions, whether he wants to or not. Some shape-shifters may shift their entire bodies, or may only shift individual parts of the body, and some can shift partly into animal form while retaining some of their human form. Shape-shifters also have varying degrees of mental control while shifted; some retain their human minds and complete control over their actions, and others are taken over by the animal and retain none of their human mind or the ability to control their actions.

Mental Shape-Shifting

The most common kind of shape-shifter is the mental shape-shifter. These are people who deliberately enter a trance state in order to "become" an animal. This is most common among shamans and religious animists. These shamans do not transform physically, but can go deeply into a trance state in which they commune with an animal spirit, sometimes so much so that they believe they are inhabited by the spirit of the animal. In such a state they may behave very much like the animal they have "shifted" into. This is usually done to enhance the shaman's understanding of the animal or to gain some power or ability from it.

Shamans are no more dangerous than any other person. Under normal circumstances, a shape-shifting shaman is not a danger, but a boon to the community. A good shaman is like any other clergy-person and often has counseling or healing abilities. Also, most shamans are aware that their behavior reflects on all other shamans, so they tend to work harder than most at being upstanding citizens. However, as there are bad people in this world, so can there be bad shamans who might use their abilities and insight to do harm. But even in a worst-case scenario, such a shaman would be no more dangerous than any other intelligent and insightful person.

An interesting historical account of mental shape-shifting is the case of the Viking Berserkers. These were fierce warriors who donned the skins of animals, often wolves or bears, to imbue themselves with the animal's strength and ferocity. They were believed to howl like wolves during battle and to drink the blood of slain enemies to gain further strength. In some legends, Berserkers are even able to make a physical transformation into the animal whose skins were worn, though that is unlikely to have been true. Such stories were no doubt encouraged in order to enhance the Berserkers' ferocious reputation.

Also, there is a rare form of lunacy known as lycanthropy, in which people believe themselves to be werewolves or other physical shape-shifters. Such people truly believe themselves to shift their physical forms, and often perform unspeakable violence as a result. Like many of the clinically insane, they show tremendous physical strength and exhibit no signs of having any real control over their actions.

Malignant Magick

PHYSICAL SHAPE-SHIFTING

A far more rare form of shape-shifter is the one who physically transforms. This transformation may be only partial, resulting in a man-creature, or total, in which the shifter looks like the animal (but perhaps larger). This type of shape-shifting may be voluntary or involuntary.

There are several ways in which people become physical shape-shifters. If the transformation is voluntary, it is often the result of magick. In lore, this can be done through magickal talismans—often belts or skins of the animal—or through spells and ritual. For example, in stories of the Loup-Garou, the French werewolf, a person must find and wear an enchanted belt in order to turn into a large, powerful wolf. While transformed, the Loup-Garou maintains a human mind and has complete control over his or her actions. In stories of the Runaturunco of Argentina, the person involved is a sorcerer who performs a ritual that imbues him with the ability to take on the form of any animal once the sun goes down.

Stories are also told of involuntary shape-shifting. The most famous example of this is the modern werewolf, which may either shift whenever it likes—as long as it happens regularly—or will shift on the evening of the full moon or the three days surrounding it. These shape-shifters can physically transform either into wolf-men, true wolves—or both. While in wolf-man form they are often very strong, heal quickly, and may or may not retain their human intelligence and will. While in wolf form they may or may not be stronger than a normal wolf their size, may or may not have superhuman senses and healing abilities, and may or may not retain human intelligence or will.

In modern stories, werewolves are created through heredity, bites, or curses. A hereditary werewolf is born when the father is a werewolf. The mother is almost always human, as most stories state that a pregnant shifter would lose her child if she changed form. The most common way werewolves are made in modern stories is via bites or sometimes scratches; really anything that involves exposure to "infected" blood. The recipient of the bite will transform, either immediately or at the next full moon. In some very rare cases, a person can be cursed into shape-shifting, such as in the tale of the Children of Lir, in which a jealous mother turns her children into swans for 300 years. (For a complete telling of the story visit *www.ireland-information.com/articles/thechildrenoflir.htm.*)

DEFENSE AGAINST THE DARK

Many legendary shape-shifters are creatures that were never human. Creatures such as Kelpies, Kitsune, Naga, and Ilimu are supernatural creatures that have the ability to shape-shift into human form for their own purposes. In most cases, shape-shifting creatures transform into humans to gather intelligence, to seduce, or to lead people astray—often to their dooms. The Ilimu of Kenya are evil spirits that possess animals (most often lions), and can shape-shift into human form by obtaining hair or blood from a person. The Ilimu then shifts into an exact replica of that person, often killing him and taking his place. In this way, the Ilimu infiltrates human society in order to select, befriend, and isolate its victim. Once it has isolated its chosen victim, the Ilimu will revert to its animal form and kill and eat its prey.

METHODS OF REMOVAL
MENTAL SHAPE-SHIFTERS

Most mental shape-shifters pose absolutely no threat to anyone, and therefore no action need be taken against them. In the extremely rare case of an insane and dangerous mental shape-shifter, the proper authorities should be alerted to the danger to the community.

PHYSICAL SHAPE-SHIFTERS

Physical shape-shifters are extremely rare. The only ones you are ever likely to encounter (and it's quite unlikely at that) are those that are supernatural creatures posing as humans. It is extremely difficult to discern whether someone who appears human is actually something else. You may feel a sense of uneasiness around the "person," he or she may seem disconnected with reality, his or her eyes may change color or shape, or he or she may do things that seem somehow superhuman. These types of things may be signs that the person is unnatural, or he or she might be having a bad day or suffer from some illness. Unless you actually witness someone changing his or her shape, or you have excellent metaphysical senses, there's no way to really know.

If you think someone might be a supernatural creature simply appearing as a human, be wary and alert in that person's presence. Use good judgment. If he or she suggests something dangerous or foolish, just decline, as you would with any other person making such a suggestion. If you feel the need, do an unobtrusive personal protection ritual when that person is around (detailed in Part II). There's little else to be done.

If you think someone is a human shape-shifter, take care. Some people are good and some people are not; treat them accordingly. Silver is known to repel or even harm shape-shifters, and in some lore, prayers or blessings do the same. Take the kind of physical precautions you would in the presence of any person you were unsure of or thought might be dangerous.

In the extremely unlikely event that you are attacked by a shape-shifter in animal form, you will need to physically protect yourself. Use common sense in this kind of situation. If a large animal is attacking you, run away if you can and get yourself to safety. Call for help. If you can't get away, you may have to fight. In some lore silver bullets (or any bullets) will drop a shape-shifter. Once again, use common sense. If an unusually large wolf is bearing down on you, does it really matter whether you think it might be a shape-shifter? Do what you need to do to keep yourself safe.

Thoughtform

VITAL STATISTICS
Danger Level: 6
Rarity: 6
Difficulty of Removal: 6
Where Found: Near magickal practitioners.
Common Symptoms: Feeling a presence in an otherwise unoccupied space, hearing a disembodied voice, objects moving of their own accord, unexplained shadows, movement out of the corner of the eye, feelings of being watched.

LORE

Thoughtforms, also called Servitors and Egregores, bridge the gap between magick and creatures of the night. They are a concentration of magickal energy created by a magickal practitioner for a particular purpose and imbued with a certain degree of independence.

Thoughtforms can achieve similar purposes as spells. A spell is essentially energy that a practitioner charges with a particular intent and then sends out into the world in order to manifest. For example, a practitioner might do a spell to help him- or herself remember important information. The energy of the spell would then help the practitioner remember. The difference between a thoughtform and a spell is that a thoughtform has some amount of independence from the practitioner.

The act of creating a thoughtform is a very advanced form of magick. To create a thoughtform, a practitioner will raise energy and imbue it with their intent. For example, a practitioner may create a thoughtform to help identify a useful book that is hidden among many books. The practitioner would raise energy and imbue it with the intent to find the book and make it stand out so that the practitioner can find it. The thoughtform would then, on its own, seek out that book. Unlike a spell, the thoughtform has enough independence to choose how it will go about finding the correct book and has enough intelligence to evaluate the books it examines. A thoughtform would have enough intelligence to think of looking in other rooms than, say, the library, and enough independence to do so. A spell works much more literally, doing exactly what the practitioner has specified—no more and no less. This gives thoughtforms tremendous versatility as a magickal tool.

At creation, the practitioner should give the thoughtform an expiration date, after which the thoughtform should be dispelled or otherwise laid to rest. While they are accomplishing their goals, thoughtforms are no danger to anyone, unless their goal is malevolent. The problem with beneficial thoughtforms comes if they are not dispelled once their task is complete. Thoughtforms have a certain degree of intelligence, more

Malignant Magick

or less depending on how they are created, and they grow stronger the longer they exist. This can lead to a thoughtform growing to become a dangerous entity. Further, if neglected by the practitioner that created it, a thoughtform can develop its own personality and its own whims in time; an entity with power, personality, desires, and independence can do whatever it wants, for good or ill. Oftentimes, a neglected thoughtform will engage in goblin-like behavior: moving objects, tripping people, and so on. (For a more detailed description of goblin-like behaviors, see the entry on goblins.) There are enough mischievous and malevolent creatures in the world; we don't need ones of our own making. If a practitioner gives the thoughtform automatic expiration conditions, then this danger never arises.

While under the control of a practitioner, thoughtforms are as good or bad as the goals to which they are set. Unfortunately, a thoughtform can be used to the same effect as a curse. It is possible, though highly unethical, to create a thoughtform and give it the purpose of harassing or harming someone. Under those circumstances, a thoughtform could have almost any negative symptom imaginable. The only way to differentiate between a negative thoughtform and other malevolent entities would be to look at the breadth of the symptoms. If the victim experiences a vast array of negative symptoms that would normally require the attentions of several negative entities, then a thoughtform is the most likely answer, because having several different kinds of negative entities in one place is virtually unheard of—negative entities do not play well with each other. Fortunately, negative thoughtforms are rare and they can be addressed in ways that would also address most of the other creatures that could be causing the symptoms.

METHODS OF REMOVAL

The most appropriate way to deal with a thoughtform depends on whether it is undispelled or intentionally malevolent. Undispelled thoughtforms can usually be dealt with by smudging or doing a simple banishing. (Both of these methods are described in detail in Part II.) If that fails, then a strong banishing can be attempted. That should deal with all but the strongest of thoughtforms. However, if a thoughtform has been left on its own for many years, it can grow to the point that even a strong banishing may fail. Under those rare circumstances, an advanced magickal practitioner should be sought for help. Then the advanced practitioner can modify the ritual *To Dispel an Errant Elemental*, presented in the section on Elementals, to dispel the thoughtform.

Dealing with an intentionally malevolent thoughtform is a bit simpler. One can treat the situation in the same way one deals with curses. A basic hex-breaking ritual should remove most negative thoughtforms, and a strong hex-breaking should deal with stronger thoughtforms. The rituals "Elemental Hex Breaking" and "Strong Hex-Breaking" presented in Part II should be sufficient. Should both of those rituals fail, then follow the instructions for dispelling an Elemental to dispel the thoughtform.

Part II

Magickal Protection

In this half of the book you will be introduced to various spells, rituals, and other methods of defending oneself from both malicious magick and creatures of the night—such as everything described in Part I. When used appropriately, these methods are quite effective at magickal self-defense. They do assume a certain familiarity with the basic mechanics of magickal practice; once again, if you are unfamiliar with defensive magick I strongly suggest you find one of the many books dedicated to the basics of magick. I particularly like *Magickal Self-Defense: A Quantum Approach to Warding* by Kerr Cuhulain, and *Protection & Reversal Magick: A Witch's Defense Manual* by Jason Miller.

- 7 -

Basic Protection

DEFENSE AGAINST THE DARK

This chapter details several fundamental methods of magickal protection all practitioners should know. It includes basic defensive preparation, an introduction to shielding, and an introduction to dimming (using magick to hide in plain sight). Under *Defensive Preparation*, you'll learn how to heighten your magickal awareness using the Quick Defensive Preparation, and how to quiet and focus the mind through grounding and centering. Under *Shielding*, you'll learn the fundamentals of creating a magickal barrier to protect yourself from negative energy. Under *Dimming*, you'll learn how keep yourself from being noticed by malevolent entities. These easy and versatile techniques will serve to protect you in everyday life and against the less powerful and more common negative entities detailed in the field guide.

DEFENSIVE PREPARATION
QUICK DEFENSIVE PREPARATION

Whenever you feel the need to be on your guard, do the following exercise.

- ◎ *Take a deep breath, in and out.*
- ◎ *Take a deep breath in and feel all the stress in your body vibrating like static electricity. Forcefully breathe out and see the stress rush out of your body and into the ground like a torrent of water.*
- ◎ *Breathe in and visualize a sphere of calm silver energy in the center of your body. Breathe out and see it expand until it forms a sphere around you.*
- ◎ *Breathe in and let your mind be still. Breathe out.*

The whole exercise should take the time of four breaths. If it takes you longer than that, you'll need to practice until you can do it quickly. This exercise should make you feel calm and focused.

GROUNDING AND CENTERING

Grounding and centering is a way of connecting yourself to the energy around you. It is vital to be grounded and centered before doing any ritual or magick; otherwise you will find yourself completely drained when it's over. When you are grounded and centered the energy around

156

you flows through you with ease. Thus, any energy you raise will be from nature and not from your personal energy.

Grounding is the act of flushing out any negative energy you have. The easiest way to do this is to think of all of your negative energy as black splotches in your aura. Then see all of it begin to drain towards your feet and then down into the ground where it is absorbed and sucked away.

Centering is connecting yourself to the energy around you. To do this, imagine two swirls of light, one silver and floating above your head; the other gold and swirling below your feet. Imagine the two swirls of light slowly spiraling towards the center of your body, filling you with energy. When they meet in the center, your entire body is engulfed in energy. The light fades, but you are still connected to all of the energy of the cosmos.

A Boosting Ritual

Here is a short ritual that you may find helpful for giving your magick a boost. It is particularly useful when done before a larger protection ritual.

- *Ground and center as usual. See the four elements around you, with yourself as the center.*

- *Feel the power of the north, the power of earth, flow through you, growing up from the ground, bringing you strength, stability, and grounding.*

- *Feel the power of the east, power of air, like wind flowing through you, bringing you wisdom, communication, and inspiration.*

- *Feel the power of the south, the power of fire, burn through you, bringing you passion, will, and true power.*

- *Feel the power of the west, power of water, flow through you, bringing you purity, healing, and rebirth.*

- *Feel the elements dancing within you. Feel your spirit uniting with them, binding them together, uniting them in the full power of the star within you.*

- *You are flooded with the full power of nature.*

SHIELDING

Shielding is a critical defensive technique. Many, if not all, magickal practitioners have some form of shielding up at all times. The most basic shield is the bubble shield: a sphere or oval of blue-white energy that serves as a barrier between the caster and the outside world, blocking negativity. In its more advanced forms the bubble shield can act as a filter, allowing certain types of energy in while keeping others out. Infinite variations can be made on the basic bubble shield, depending on what you would like it to do.

To put up a bubble shield simply envision a white or blue egg, crackling with energy, at the center of your being. Envision that bubble expanding outward, up and down, until it surrounds your entire body. It should extend about six inches above your head and another six inches below your feet. Hold the image of the shield in the back of your mind as you go about your tasks. When you're ready to lower the shield, envision it turning into a sheet of water that opens at the top and then flows down into the ground.

Always try to do a quick grounding and centering before you shield. A good shield creates a metaphysical barrier between you and the world around you, keeping external energies out. It also keeps internal energies in. If you're filled with fear and anxiety, those feelings may become trapped in your shields, unable to drain away. Better to get rid of them through a quick grounding and centering than to let them fester. Of course, you can ground and center after you shield, but be sure to specifically visualize the energies passing through your shield and into the ground while the shield remains strong.

GROUNDING SHIELDS

Grounding shields are an excellent way to deal with everyday negativity. Instead of merely blocking negative energy, a grounding shield actually absorbs the negativity with which it comes in contact and sends it harmlessly into the earth. This type of shield is entirely benign and is appropriate in almost any circumstance.

Basic Protection

A great advantage of this type of shield is that it can actually improve the overall atmosphere of a place. When a normal filter encounters negativity, it deflects it away from you, but the negative energy is still there, hanging ominously in the environment. A grounding shield absorbs and removes negativity, making for a better environment for all present, including the one who sent out the negativity in the first place.

A further advantage of this shield is that you can make it double-sided. It can absorb and ground negativity coming toward you from the outside as well as negativity that you generate yourself. Many practitioners will configure grounding shields in this way to protect them when the people around them are having a bad day, and to protect everyone else when they're having a bad day themselves.

To cast a grounding shield:

- ◎ *Visualize yourself being encircled with brown (or whatever color you most associate with the earth) energy.*
- ◎ *Envision a lightning rod going from the bottom of the shield into the earth.*
- ◎ *Focus your intent so that it flows through the shield.*
- ◎ *Envision all negativity hitting the shield, from within or without, being drawn down the shield, into the lightning rod, and then out into the earth where it is grounded.*

To dispel a grounding shield, simply envision the entire shield melting back down into the earth.

DIMMING

This technique is appropriate for situations when the hair suddenly stands up on the back of your neck and you get the feeling that something not so nice is nearby, or is maybe even looking for you. Dimming will help you to leave a place where you feel threatened without being noticed magickally—it does nothing to make you physically invisible.

All living creatures have an aura. Very simply, your aura is your personal energy field. It can often be seen as a halo of colored light emanating from your body to about six inches from you and fading off into the distance. When feeling the area inhabited by the aura with your hands, it can feel like the air thickens and gains resistance, as opposed to the air far from the body, which does not contain a person's aura. Some negative entities are attracted to strong auras, and malevolent spells often find their targets by finding their auras. To avoid attracting this kind of attention, one can actually pull in or dim one's aura.

It can be a bit tricky at first, but will get easier with practice. It can feel uncomfortable, as though your skin is prickling or too tight. The first few times you try dimming, do not hold it for more than a few minutes at a time.

- *First, visualize your aura. If you have already learned how to see auras with either your eyes or your second sight, do so now. If not: Visualize your aura extending from your body out into the air by about six inches. You can visualize your aura in several ways; it can be the image of a halo of white light, the feel of static electricity, the smell of ozone, or whatever sensory visualization seems most natural to you.*

- *Now see/feel/smell your aura going into your body as a series of individual threads that root themselves in a ball in the center of your body.*

- *Imagine that the ball is made up of swirling, spinning energy strands like a ball of yarn.*

- *Visualize that ball turning very slowly, winding all those threads back up into the ball. Visualize the threads of your aura being very slowly pulled back in towards the center of your body, inch by inch. It is very important to do this slowly, little by little. Only contract your aura until it's about half an inch out from your skin. This will feel slightly uncomfortable, but won't hurt you. If you begin to feel lightheaded, panicky, or very uncomfortable, unwind your aura immediately.*

- *To let your aura back out, just visualize the ball of energy in the center of your body unwinding and releasing the threads of your aura back to its natural state.*

It's a good idea to ground after using this technique. I would also recommend eating something connecting you to earth, such as bread, nuts, or cheese.

Basic Protection

CHAMELEON AURA

A slightly more advanced technique is to simultaneously dim your own aura and pull on the aura of your surroundings. This is essentially being an auric chameleon. Instead of making your physical body look like your surroundings, you're making your aura look like the aura of your surroundings so that you blend into the background to anything looking at you with second sight alone.

- ◎ *First feel the energy of your surroundings. What does it feel like? Is the energy warm, cold, strong, weak, moving, sluggish, or what? There is no right answer for describing the energy of a place; just think about what it feels like to you. For example, the energy of my school feels to me like it's bright, sharp, and constantly moving.*

- ◎ *See that ambient energy like a carpet that sits over the surroundings—over the ground, the walls, furniture, and so on.*

- ◎ *Now, dim your aura as per the previous exercise.*

- ◎ *See the auric carpet of your surroundings; visualize that carpet wrapping around you, covering your own aura. See that external aura detaching from the surroundings, so that you can move around and still have it around you.*

- ◎ *When you no longer need the external aura (or if you begin to feel uncomfortable), see the auric carpet unwrapping from you and melting off, being absorbed back into the surroundings and then unwind your own aura.*

Ground after using this technique.

INVISIBILITY SPELLS

Similar to the techniques outlined for dimming, invisibility spells are designed to make you blend into the background. They will not make you physically invisible, though you may find that people walk right by you when you have them in place. All these spells do is lower your profile so you are less noticeable. Make sure you remove the spell when you want to be seen again.

INVISIBILITY SPELL

On this night and in this hour
I call upon the ancient powers of shadow and mist.
Wrap around me.
Hide me from prying eyes.
Let me fade.
Unnoticed.
Unnoted.
Unseen.
I'm not here now.
Chameleon-like, I am unseen.
Until I will to be seen again.
Never let this spell reverse
or upon me place a curse.
By nature's will and harm to none
Let this my spell not be undone.

REVERSAL

My spell is done
From it I wean.
Reveal me now
I can be seen.

– 8 –

Tools

Defense Against the Dark

In this chapter you will learn to create the tools that will enable you to protect yourself and others against almost any negative magick or entity. You will learn how to create both holy water and war water for use in cleansings and banishings, as well as how to use various salts in the same. You will also learn how to make and use Witch Bottles—magickal containers for trapping and neutralizing negative energy. This section also lists common herbs, stones, and oils that can be used to enhance any protective magickal working. You will learn the fundamentals of smudging—the use of smoldering herbs to clear negative energy from a person or place. You will also learn the versatile techniques of using mojos (bags of magickally charged materials) and energy balls to cleanse objects and places, and even banish negative entities. Learn to wield these magickal tools with precision and you will be effectively armed against all but the most fearsome of malevolent entities.

Water

Water is the ultimate cleanser and is used in many cleansing and protective spells and rituals. Although any water will do, it's nice to have something with a little more oomph. Salt water is the easiest and most common protective water around. If you live near a large body of salt water, then you've got an infinite supply of naturally charged protective water. If you live inland, you can add salt to tap water and get something just as good.

The most well-known protective water is holy water. Holy water can be used to cleanse and protect people, objects, and places, making it useful in virtually any defensive situation. Traditionally, holy water is made via a blessing by a Catholic priest who truly believes in what he is doing. If you have access to such water, by all means use it. However, if you don't have access to or feel uncomfortable using such water, you can make your own. If you are a person of faith, it may be best for you to create holy water by praying to your deity and asking him or her to bless a bowl of water.

Here is a way for anyone to create blessed protective water:

Tools

◎ *Fill a bowl with water and place it either on the floor or on your altar.*

◎ *Hold your hands a few inches above the water and visualize bright white light gathering from the air into the palms of your hands.*

◎ *Say:*

Bright purifying waters cleanse and protect. Wash away negativity and strife. Bring peace and calm in your wake. Bright purifying waters cleanse and protect.

◎ *Lower your hands to the surface of the water and visualize the white light flowing into the water in the bowl until the water shines with energy.*

◎ *Say:*

My spell is done.

Now you can bottle the water and put it in your kit.

Slightly less well-known is war water. War water is **very potent** water that can be used for aggressive cleansings, protection from malevolent entities, and curse reversal. To make war water, you need a jar with a tight-fitting lid (old mason jars work perfectly) and some cut iron nails (these can be obtained for pennies at any hardware store). Put the nails in the jar and cover them with water. Seal the lid and wait until the nails begin to rust—usually a week or so. Once the water turns a rusty red-orange color you've got war water. As you use the water, more plain water can be added to the jar until the nails have completely disintegrated. To use the water, just put it in vials in your kit and sprinkle it where it's needed.

SALT

Salt may be the perfect protective tool; it's non-toxic, inexpensive, and incredibly common. Salt can be sprinkled over a person, rubbed on an object, or sprinkled around a room to cleanse and purify.

A word on salt outdoors: salt is potent stuff and it can kill plants. As a result, you do not want to use normal salt in gardens or other outdoor spaces. When doing defensive work outdoors, try using Epsom salts ($MgSO_4$) instead of normal salt ($NaCl$). Epsom salts magickally function similarly to normal salts, will not harm plant life, and can be purchased at any drug store.

THE WITCH BOTTLE

The Witch Bottle is one of the easiest and most potent forms of defense for use in the home. The idea behind the Witch Bottle is to create a simulacrum that tricks negative energy into thinking it has found its target, and then trapping it—permanently. Witch Bottles are particularly useful when doing house cleansings or hex-breaking.

To create a Witch Bottle you will need a jar or bottle with a tight-fitting screw-on lid and lots of sharp, unpleasant things (tacks, needles, briars, rusty nails, wood splinters, and so on), and some duct tape. Fill the jar with the sharp and unpleasant things and screw on the lid. In that state, it can sit in your kit until you need it.

BE CAREFUL when handling all those sharp things; it is very easy to cut yourself. It's not a bad idea to have some disinfectant and band-aids handy when making Witch Bottles. Many of these items can cause tetanus if they puncture the skin. Make sure that your tetanus shots are up to date.

When you're ready to use the Witch Bottle you can open the jar and personalize it in this way: Fill the jar up about halfway with water, and put in some hair or fingernail clippings of the person or persons being protected. Then close the lid as tightly as possible, sealing it with duct tape. Traditionally, the jar would then be buried on the person's property, often near the front door or in the garden. If you can bury the jar somewhere it is unlikely to ever be disturbed, do so. If not, the jar can also be placed in the back corner of a closet or in a seldom-used drawer.

PROTECTIVE HERBS, STONES, AND OILS

Common protective herbs:

- ☆ Angelica
- ☆ Bay leaves
- ☆ Blackberry leaves
- ☆ Cinnamon
- ☆ Cloves
- ☆ Comfrey
- ☆ Fennel
- ☆ Garlic
- ☆ Juniper berries
- ☆ Mullein
- ☆ Rosemary
- ☆ Rue
- ☆ Sage
- ☆ Vetiver

Common protective stones:

- ☆ Agate
- ☆ Amber
- ☆ Amethyst
- ☆ Black tourmaline
- ☆ Bloodstone
- ☆ Garnet
- ☆ Hematite
- ☆ Jade
- ☆ Jet
- ☆ Malachite
- ☆ Obsidian

☆ Tiger's eye

☆ Quartz

☆ Salt

Protective Oils:

☆ Essential oils from any of the herbs listed previously.

☆ Dragon's blood oil—made from tree resin.

☆ Fiery Wall of Protection oil—a blend of equal parts salt, dragon's blood, frankincense, and myrrh. To make the oil, put approximately two tablespoons of salt into a mortar. Add to this three drops each of dragon's blood, frankincense, and myrrh oils. Blend with a pestle until you have a paste. Then add as much jojoba or olive oil as necessary to make the resulting liquid pourable.

☆ Basic protection oil—a blend of equal parts peppermint, cinnamon, rue, and vervain essential oils in a jojoba base. To make the oil, put at least two tablespoons of jojoba oil in a container. Add two drops each of peppermint, cinnamon, rue, and vervain oils. Mix together. *Do not add more than two drops each of the essential oils.* These are potent oils and can irritate the skin in high concentrations.

SMUDGING

Smudging is the burning of dried herbs to create a cleansing smoke bath, which is used to purify people, ceremonial and ritual space, and ceremonial tools and objects. As the herbs smolder, the smoke is taken in one's hands and rubbed over the body, area, or object. It is sometimes also wafted in a similar manner, usually by feathers dressed in a ceremonial manner, for the express purpose of smudging.

Smudging is the common name given to the Sacred Smoke Bowl Blessing, a powerful cleansing technique from the Native American tradition. Smudging calls on the spirits of sacred plants to drive away negative energies and return you to a state of balance. It is the psychic equivalent of washing your hands. It is commonly used as a ritual for cleansing, purifying, and protecting the physical and spiritual bodies of people, places, and objects.

Many differing cultures and peoples have their own methods and herbal mixtures for this purpose. Not everyone views the practice of smudging in the same way, and different herbs may be used for different purposes. Some herbs used traditionally are sage, cedar or juniper, lavender, and sweet grass. Generally, sage, sweet grass, and cedar are burned to purify and protect one's living area, self, and sacred tools. Pure tobacco is also used by some Plains tribes, and copal is used in South and Central America. The herbs can be burnt on their own or in mixtures, depending on tradition and required effect.

To perform a traditional Native American smudging ceremony, burn a combination of dried sage, cedar, and sweet grass. This is most easily done by letting the herbs smolder on a piece of charcoal or in a fireproof dish of some kind. Rub your hands in the smoke, and then gather the smoke and bring it into your body or rub it onto yourself, especially any area you feel needs spiritual healing. Focus your intent on the energy of the plants cleansing your spirit. To perform the ceremony for another person, simply change where the smoke goes.

Mojos

A mojo is a simple and versatile protective object. You can use any scrap of material large enough to be gathered into a pouch shape, and you can fill it with just about anything. Mojo bags are commonly made out of cotton (such as cotton tea bags, usually found in the organic section of most supermarkets), but can be made out of any fabric, or even materials such as plastic wrap or aluminum foil, in a pinch.

The filling in a mojo can be anything that has sympathetic qualities to the intended purpose. Mojos tend to work best when they only have three to five small items in them, which keeps the energy focused, although they can have any number of items in them. A good example of a protective mojo might be a small cotton bag holding a lock of the target's hair tied with a red ribbon, a piece of garnet anointed with Fiery Wall of Protection oil, a bit of ash from the target's hearth (or dirt from near his or her door, or dust from someplace where he or she spends a lot of time), and a small sprig of rosemary. In this example the hair and the ash identify who is to be protected, and the red ribbon, garnet, oil, and rosemary all have protective qualities that will be sympathetically transmitted to the target. This mojo could either be personally carried by the target (in a pocket or bag) or placed in the target's home.

To create a mojo, first gather your materials so that everything you need is at hand. Then ground and center yourself. Look at each of the items and think about their significance. Place the container (bag) on the ground so that you can easily put the filling inside. Pick up the first item and say, "I add [name of item] for [purpose, for example to identify the target or to impart protection]." Do this for each item until the mojo is full. Then seal the mojo (by tying, taping, or otherwise closing the pouch), and say "Protection brought, protection bring, to [target's name or "whomever holds thee"] for one moon. So mote it be."

Like many small magickal objects, mojos have a limited lifespan. A typical mojo will last about one moon cycle and then fade. However, you can shorten or lengthen their useful life by specifically charging them to last during a set time period. For example, instead of charging a mojo to last "for one moon," you could charge it to last "from March 3rd to May 3rd," or some other set time period.

Another way to lengthen a mojo's lifespan is to recharge it. At the end of the mojo's set time you can unseal the pouch, remove the contents, cleanse them, and then re-create the mojo. If any fresh herbs were used in the original mojo, they should be replaced with new ones. Also, any oils used should be reapplied. By remaking it, the mojo will be re-energized for another set period.

When you are done with the mojo, you can bury it or disassemble it and cleanse the materials. If the mojo contained non-perishable items, such as stones, they can potentially be reused after a good cleansing.

ENERGY BALLS

Strictly speaking, energy balls are more of a technique than a tool. However, you may not have your kit on you at all times. Tools are helpful and can make doing magick easier, but the tools themselves do not produce magick—you do. If you're conscious, you can make an energy ball, and if you can make an energy ball you can probably do whatever magick is necessary in a given situation.

An energy ball is a concentration of energy in a small, manageable size. Although usually made as a small sphere, it can actually be of any easily visualized shape. Energy balls are extremely versatile. Virtually any type of energy can be gathered into a ball for easy use. For example, healing energy can be gathered into a ball and lowered into a person to be healed, or lowered into a candle to charge it for a spell. We'll focus on protective and cleansing energy balls here.

How do I make one?

As with most magick, first you ground and center. You must connect to outside energies before gathering the energy for a ball, or the ball will be created out of your own energies and can drain you dry.

Once properly grounded and centered, hold your hands in front of you, palms facing each other. Hold your hands as close together as is necessary (but not touching each other) until you can feel energy flowing between them.

Once you can feel energy flowing between your palms, mentally increase the energy flow. Visualize the energy around you flowing into you, through you, and into the space between your palms. As you pull this energy into a ball, think about your intent (protection, cleansing, and so on). Visualize the energy taking on the characteristics of your intent. See it take on the proper color, shape, size, and texture (a protective ball may be white and spiky, whereas a cleansing ball may be blue and fluid—it all depends on how you believe it should be).

Once the ball is of the correct size and character for your purpose, stop gathering further energies. Visualize the energy flowing around and around in the ball you have created. The energy ball should feel thick and should offer some resistance if you try to move your hands closer together (like squeezing a balloon). If you look into the center of the ball the air should seem thicker there, and it may look almost foggy.

How do I use one?

There are many ways to use an energy ball. Objects can be charged by lowering the ball onto them or raising the object into the ball. The ball can also be placed into a person (with his or her express consent, of course), as is often done in healing.

How do I dispel one?

If you accidentally make your ball too big or you don't want to use it anymore, visualize some of the energy spooling off and going into the ground (or a handy crystal) until the ball is the correct size or totally drained away.

- 9 -

Protective Charms and Incantations

This chapter lists several useful charms and incantations for common scenarios. It includes a basic incantation suitable for any situation, a basic travel safety incantation, a magick charm to alert you to incoming dangers, a charm you can physically create and carry with you to ward off danger, and instructions for seeking aid from protective entities. Potent as they are, the effectiveness of these charms and incantations can be increased by personalizing them in a way that resonates with whomever is using them. For example, to personalize the Simple Protective Incantation you might envision the sphere of energy as being red or black or some other color that you feel symbolizes protection. Experiment and see what works best for you.

Simple Protective Incantation

Here is a simple protective incantation that you can say, either aloud or in your head. While envisioning yourself being surrounded by a sphere of protective energy, say:

> *Safe within the circle round thrice sealed, thrice bound.*
> *Safe within the circle round thrice sealed, thrice bound.*
> *Safe within the circle round thrice sealed, thrice bound.*

Travel Safety Incantation

This incantation is most effective when said before one sets off on a journey, and can be repeated at any time during the journey to boost its effectiveness.

> *By the powers of the moon and sun, I conjure.*
> *I travel this night.*
> *Great power of the west,*
> *Guardian of travelers,*
> *Watch over me.*
> *Keep me safe, sane, and sound.*
> *I will depart on time.*
> *I will arrive on time.*

Protective Charms and Incantations

My road will know no obstacles.

My journey will know no hardships.

Let my lessons from this journey be brief.

I will fly like the wind,

Where I want to go.

I meet those who care, safely.

Thus do I conjure.

WATCHDOG CHARM

This is a simple charm to enhance your magickal senses and have them alert you when something potentially threatening comes near you. This charm does not act as a protection charm, but only alerts you of the potential threat so that you can assess it and deal with it appropriately.

◎ *Envision the air around you beginning to move clockwise around your body.*

◎ *Say:*

Power of air encircle me, all incoming danger you will see, when danger comes by alert me, as I do will so mote it be.

When activated, this charm will "tug" at you to let you know that it senses a threat. You may feel this as a physical tug, a feeling of discomfort at the base of your spine, or perhaps an odd itch (I tend to feel it as though someone's pulling on a string attached to my lower back). It may take you a few times before you start to recognize the charm's "tug," but once you do it, is very useful.

PROTECTIVE CHARM

Get some oven-hardening clay and fashion it into a flat disk. Inscribe a Celtic knot on one side of the disk and a pentacle (or other protective symbol) on the other. Bake this as instructed on the clay package. Charge the knot so that any negative energy coming your way gets sucked into the knot where it can't do any harm. An easy way to charge an item is to focus on your intent (for example, repelling negativity or gaining protection) while holding the item. Gather your will and intent into your hands and let it flow into the item. Then charge the pentacle with protective energy. Carry this with you at all times.

PROTECTIVE ENTITIES

The following list of protective entities consists of those that are generally friendly to anyone and will usually be willing to lend their aid. However, these are sentient beings and may or may not agree to help you at any given time. Treat them with respect. Also, many protective entities prefer to work in specific contexts, for example protecting children against illness or protecting young men at war. Researching specific entities before you call on them to learn their preferences in this area is always advised.

Common protective entities:

☆ Athena

☆ Kwan Yin

☆ Oya

☆ Ares

☆ Shango

☆ Archangel Michael

☆ Isis

☆ Zhong Kui

☆ Thor

☆ Morrighan

Protective Charms and Incantations

Incantation for Seeking Aid

Here is a simple incantation for seeking aid from a protective entity. You can certainly use it to call upon the entities just listed, but it is most effective if you have already established a working relationship with the entity in question. If you are religious, a prayer or evocation to your deity in the manner in which it is accustomed to being called will be more effective than the following incantation.

O Great [entity's name], hear me! I call upon you for protection, for I have great need!

I am threatened and need your aid. Please watch over me and protect me.

When the danger has passed, be sure to thank the entity for its aid. It would also be appropriate to make some kind of offering, such as incense or food, in its name as thanks.

- 10 -
Cleansing and Protective Rituals

DEFENSE AGAINST THE DARK

This chapter gives detailed instruction on how to perform cleansing and protective rituals for various situations. For each ritual herein I have provided guidelines for how and when to use it, lists of materials necessary, and explicit instructions for how to perform it. Be sure to read the ritual thoroughly before attempting to perform it. Be certain that you understand all the steps required and you are comfortable performing them. If you are not comfortable with *any* of the steps in a ritual, do not perform it. Also, make sure that you have all your materials gathered before you begin, and ensure you will not be interrupted once you've started—tell others what you're doing and not to disturb you, and turn off your cell phone. If the ritual involves open flame, such as a candle, be sure to have a bucket of water or a fire extinguisher handy. Safety first!

PERSONAL PROTECTION
UNOBTRUSIVE PROTECTION RITUAL

This ritual is for use when you are in public or any situation in which you do not want anyone around you to realize that you are doing magick. It is appropriate for any situation in which there is negativity in the air or you feel uncomfortable. This ritual is good for preventing yourself from being targeted by a negative entity, but is unlikely to stop an attack once it's begun. It is also an excellent ritual to do in conjunction with the auric dimming described in Chapter 7.

Before doing this ritual, find a simple protection symbol that appeals to you, such as a pentagram, cross, or the Tiwaz rune (↑). The symbol can be anything simple as long as it feels protective to you.

- ⊚ *Begin by taking a deep breath, and then ground and center.*
- ⊚ *Envision the protective symbol you've chosen. Trace the shape of that symbol on each of your palms with the opposite hand.*
- ⊚ *Envision yourself growing hard overlapping scales all over your body until you are completely covered. You can still move freely, but the scales deflect negative energy like armor.*
- ⊚ *When you feel you no longer need it, envision the scales absorbing back into your skin.*

Cleansing and Protective Rituals

GIRDING RITUAL

This is a strong personal protection ritual and is excellent to do before confronting a known negative entity, or before any situation in which you think it likely that strong negative energy will be deliberately directed at you. This ritual will be most effective if you have a relationship with a protective entity or deity. If you do not, simply skip that step.

◎ *Begin by taking a few deep, calming breaths. Then ground and center.*

◎ *Envision a shield of stone forming in front of you. Say:*

Shield of stone, absorb all negativity directed at me.
Absorb it and send it into the earth where it can do no harm.
Shield of stone, lend me the strength and firmness of the earth,
that none may do me harm.

◎ *Now envision that shield growing around you until it surrounds you in a sphere of stone.*

◎ *Envision a shield of fire forming behind you. Say:*

Shield of fire, protect me from harm.
Absorb all anger and hatred directed towards me and burn it to nothing.
Shield of fire, give me strength of will and fierceness,
that none may defeat me.

◎ *Now envision that shield growing around you until it surrounds you in a sphere of fire.*

◎ *Envision a shield of wind forming to your right. Say:*

Shield of wind, blow away all that is baneful.
Blow away negativity and malice, scatter it to the four winds so that it may do no harm.
Shield of wind, keep me alert and give me wisdom,
that I may choose well in the clinch.

◎ *Now envision that shield growing around you until it surrounds you in a sphere of wind.*

◎ *Envision a shield of water forming to your left. Say:*

Shield of water, wash away all that is baneful.
Wash away negativity and malice, let it dissolve so that it may do no harm.
Shield of water, heal my mind, body, and soul,
that I may face the world hale and strong.

◎ *Now envision that shield growing around you until it surrounds you in a sphere of water.*

◎ *Take a deep breath and feel yourself surrounded and infused with the powers of stone, fire, wind, and water.*

If you do not have a working relationship with a protective entity, skip this next step.

◎ *Think of the protective entity that you work with and say:*

[Entity], friend of mine. Be with me this day/night.
Protect and watch over me, so that I will succeed in my endeavor.
Blessed Be.

When you've accomplished your task, thank your protective entity as you normally do. Then envision each of your shields dissipating back to its element—stone would turn to dust, wind would blow away, and so on.

SLEEP PROTECTION SPELL

This is an effective spell best done just before bed. Any of the spoken lines may be said aloud or silently, making it suitable even when you're not alone.

Cleansing and Protective Rituals

◎ *Ground and center.*

◎ *Chant:*

> *Safe within the circle round, thrice sealed, thrice bound.*
> *Safe within the circle round, thrice sealed, thrice bound.*
> *Safe within the circle round, thrice sealed, thrice bound.*

◎ *Visualize a circle forming in the north and growing to encompass you. Say:*

> *With the power of Earth I banish any entity intending me harm.*
> *Nothing intending me harm may pass this ward.*
> *Earth, ground me and hide me from any that would do me harm.*

◎ *Visualize a circle forming in the east and growing to encompass you. Say:*

> *With the power of Air I banish any entity intending me harm.*
> *Nothing intending me harm may pass this ward.*
> *Air, alert me to any incoming danger and make me wise.*

◎ *Visualize a circle forming in the south and growing to encompass you. Say:*

> *With the power of Fire I banish any entity intending me harm.*
> *Nothing intending me harm may pass this ward.*
> *Fire to protect me and make me strong.*

◎ *Visualize a circle forming in the west and growing to encompass you. Say:*

> *With the power of Water I banish any entity intending me harm.*
> *Nothing intending me harm may pass this ward.*
> *Water to heal me, mind, body, and soul, and strengthen my correct intuition.*

◎ *Take a deep breath and say:*

> *By my will the circles are sealed.*
> *My circles of protection will hold until I get up tomorrow morning.*
> *So mote it be.*

Object Cleansing and Blessing

When a new object comes into someone's possession, it can sometimes contain residual energy from its previous owner, its place of manufacture, or the store where it was sold. At times, this energy can negatively affect the new owner and will need to be cleansed.

This is an ideal time to use the energy balls presented in the Chapter 8. Simply create a ball of purifying energy that is slightly larger than the object being cleansed and move the ball so that it encompasses the object. Then envision the purifying energy being absorbed by the object until the object is cleansed and fresh. Then create another energy ball containing the kind of energy the owner would like the object to have, and let the object absorb that positive energy.

House/Area Cleansing and Protection
Basic House Cleansing

For the basic house cleansing, you will need the following: as many willing participants as you can get (children are fantastic participants), pots, pans, noisemakers, squeaky toys, and anything you can find that makes annoying sounds.

Do this ritual during the middle of the day.

Arm each participant with something that makes noise—the more annoying the better. Instruct them to run through the house, yelling, laughing, and generally making as much noise as possible. Have them run around the yard, and through every room, go into cupboards and closets, attics, basements, and crawlspaces (if this is possible). Leave no quiet refuge anywhere. Spend no less than a full 10 minutes making an awful racket.

Cleansing and Protective Rituals

After you've been sufficiently obnoxious, have everyone gather in the center of the home and have the home owners link hands and say, "This is OUR house and we're not going anywhere. If you don't like it then YOU can leave."

Then throw a party for all of the participants and have as much fun as possible.

STRONG HOUSE CLEANSING

This ritual is for when the basic cleansing doesn't fix the problem. If at all possible, this ritual should be preceded by thoroughly, physically cleaning the house. Dust and clutter are great repositories of stale energy and can impede the effectiveness of energy work.

For this ritual, any non-magickal folk should leave the premises.

You will need: salt, holy water (or war water if the situation is *really* bad), a Witch Bottle, and a bell. If you don't have a bell, a portable music player with speakers is good, and any music with light, clear tones will work.

Prepare the Witch Bottle by adding hair or fingernail clippings from each member of the household. Seal the bottle with duct tape. Prepare a permanent home for the Witch Bottle—if it's going to be buried outside, dig the hole; if it's going in the back of a closet, make sure you can get to the back of the closet.

Find the heart of the home; this will be whatever area of the home people use most often—usually the kitchen or family room. In this room, stage your supplies so that they are ready for use. If you wish to set up a formal altar, do so here.

If you would like to call on any deities or other helpers, do so now.

Go to the front door and lay a line of salt across the threshold while saying: "Purifying salt, allow positive energy in and negativity out. Allow all unwanted energy and entities to leave this house, never to return." Then go clockwise around the house and lay a line of salt across the threshold of every other door that leads outside (don't forget garage doors). Then go clockwise around the house and sprinkle a few drops of holy water on every window. While doing so, envision each grain of salt and drop of water creating a continuous shield of positive energy that completely surrounds the house, with each door and window allowing negativity out, but not in.

Return to the heart of the house and firmly say: "I come this day/ night to cleanse this home. This home belongs to [home owner's name or the family's name], and negative energy and entities are unwelcome here. He/she/they want you to leave. You *shall* leave."

Then go through the house and sprinkle a few drops of holy water in *every* corner (including attics and basements if at all possible). While doing so, chant: "As I cleanse this space, negativity leaves this place." You may run across spots that seem to need more holy water than others; do give those places extra attention. *Never sprinkle holy water, or any other water, on electronics!*

Return to the heart of the house. Hold the Witch Bottle between your hands and say: "Never again shall negative energy or entities trouble [name(s) of the afflicted]. All negative energy directed to him/her/them will be trapped within this bottle where it will trouble no one. Any negative entities attempting to harm him/her/them shall be trapped within. As I will, so mote it be!"

Pick up the bell or music player and say: "As the sound of this bell/ music rings throughout this house, let it be filled with light and prosperity. Negativity be banished, let the light return!" Walk through the house ringing the bell or playing the music. If you're using the bell, ring it often enough that the tone never completely fades away. Make sure you walk through *every* room, including the garage, basement, attic, and so on. If you cannot get into the attic, basement, or crawl space, you will need to visualize the sound traveling up through the walls to fill the attic and down through the floor to fill the lowest level of the house.

Return to the heart of the house and say: "This house has been cleansed and purified. Negativity is banished. Light and prosperity fill this place. This house is now a home."

If you have called on any deities or helpers, thank and dismiss them now.

Take the Witch Bottle and put it in its permanent home.

Cleansing and Protective Rituals

BANISHING

SIMPLE BANISHING

The simplest form of banishing is to identify the entity that you wish to leave and tell it to go. You must speak firmly and confidently. If you are unsure of yourself, the entity will know it and will probably not take you seriously. If you are nervous, it's alright to have other people stand with you as you do this; a united front always gives extra strength to your words. Take a deep, calming breath and say: "[Entity], you are unwelcome here. You must go now!"

STRONG BANISHING

This form of banishing is appropriate when an entity is present in a place, is doing harm to those who live or work there, and has refused to leave when asked. The stronger a claim the occupants have on the place, the more likely this is to work; for example, a homeowner is likely to do better than someone who is house-sitting for a week.

You will need:

☆ A teaspoon to a tablespoon each of cayenne or other hot chile powder, salt, cinnamon, and sulfur powder.

☆ A small bowl.

☆ A small black candle and a small white candle.

☆ Dragon's blood oil.

☆ A small bowl of salt water (or war water if things are very bad).

Begin:

◎ *Begin by thoroughly cleaning the affected areas; every nook and cranny.*

◎ *Set up a small table in the center of the affected area.*

◎ *Carefully combine the cayenne, salt, cinnamon, and sulfur powder in a small bowl. *Do not get this in your eyes!* Go around the affected area and sprinkle this powder in the corners. As you do so, say:*

Negative entities will find no rest, no comfort here.

🌀 *Now go around to those same areas, sprinkling salt water. As you do so, say:*

Negative energy is washed from this place; negative entities will find no strength here.

🌀 *Pick up the black candle and hold it in your dominant hand. Say:*

A black candle for banishing that which is unwelcome.

🌀 *Anoint the candle with the dragon's blood oil, then sprinkle the candle with the powder you made earlier. The powder should stick to the oil.*

🌀 *Place the candle in a holder, and as you light it, say:*

As this candle burns, so are negative entities banished from this place.

🌀 *Let the black candle burn, repeating the statement once a minute for five minutes. Let the candle continue to burn until it burns out.*

🌀 *As the black candle burns, pick up the white candle with your dominant hand. Say:*

A white candle to fill the empty spaces with light and hope.

🌀 *Place the candle in a holder, and as you light it, say:*

As this candle burns, positive energy will fill this place, giving negativity no safe harbor.

🌀 *Let this candle burn out as well.*

🌀 *As the candles burn, gather your will and firmly say:*

Cleansing and Protective Rituals

All negative entities are hereby permanently banished from this place.
Let this be a place of light, hope, safety, and comfort.
This place is now blessed and nothing may dwell here uninvited.
By the power of light and flame, so mote it be!

The ritual is now over. Watch over the candles until they burn out and then bury the stubs. Let the powder sit until the next day and then vacuum it up, being sure to empty the vacuum immediately afterward.

- 11 -
Hex-Breaking

Defense Against the Dark

This chapter details two rituals for hex-breaking or curse removal. These rituals are suitable for situations in which people believe themselves to be cursed or have otherwise had negative energy attached to them. These rituals remove outside negative energy attached to the person for whom the ritual is performed. The Elemental hex-breaking is suitable for situations in which the person for whom the ritual is performed believes him- or herself to be cursed, but may or may not actually *be* cursed. It is a basic ritual that will clear negative energies that are present, but will not do any harm if there's nothing to clear. The strong hex-breaking is a more potent ritual and should be used only when there is strong evidence that the focus of the ritual is actually cursed or if the Elemental hex-breaking has failed.

One of the keys to successful hex-breaking is belief. These rituals must be performed in seriousness and with conviction to be fully effective. If the person for whom you are performing the ritual doesn't believe it will work—or worse, if *you* don't believe it will work—then it probably won't. Intent and focus are the keys to all successful magick, but they are absolutely critical to hex-breaking.

Elemental Hex-Breaking

For this ritual you will need a bowl or spritzer of salt water, a candle (tea lights work particularly well), incense or a smudge stick, a small glass of drinking water, and a small drum if you have one.

◎ *Have the hexee stand in the center of the room (or sit if it is medically necessary). Cast a circle around the person and yourself, as you normally would.*

◎ *Say:*

We come this day/night to clear [person's name] of negative influences.

Look the hexee in the eye and ask:

Is it your wish to be cleared of negative energy from within and without, and any negative influences?

192

If the person says yes, then you may continue.

◎ *Say:*

With the power of earth, we ground negativity so that it will do no harm.

Pick up the drum, hold it close to the person's head, and hit it so that the vibrations hit the person. (Warn the hexee that you will be doing this; it can be unpleasant. Also, before doing this, test it on yourself to see how loud it is. We don't want to rupture anyone's eardrums.) Next, hit the drum towards the hexee's abdomen, and then once again towards the hexee's feet. (If you do not have a drum, you can do this by clapping.) Then have the hexee turn around and repeat the three beats down the back of his or her body.

◎ *Say:*

With the power of air, we blow away negativity and bring greater awareness of it.

Pick up the smudge stick or incense and waft the smoke towards the hexee's head, abdomen, and feet. Have him or her turn around and repeat down the back of his or her body. (If the person has allergies, you can do this by simply fanning or blowing on the hexee with the same motions.)

◎ *Say:*

With the power of fire, we burn away negative influences and remove their hold.

Carefully pick up the candle and move it down the hexee's body, from head to foot. Then repeat down the back side of his or her body. Be very careful of loose clothing and hair. (If you don't have a candle or aren't comfortable with them, this can also be done with the beam of a flashlight.)

⊚ *Say:*

With the power of water, we wash away negativity and negative influences. Their hold is dissolved.

Pick up the bowl of salt water and sprinkle a few drops on top of the hexee's head, a few drops on his or her torso, and a few on his or her legs and feet. Turn the hexee around and repeat down the back of his or her body.

⊚ *Have the hexee hold the glass of water and repeat the following:*

I am blessed by the power of the elements. I am free of negativity. I am strong and protected. As I drink this water, so am I free.

Then have the hexee drink the glass of water. (He or she must drink all of it, so make it a nice small glass.)

⊚ *Close the circle as you normally would.*

STRONG HEX-BREAKING

This is for circumstances in which the previous ritual has failed. If you know specifically what is being removed, you may call it by name whenever the ritual refers to "negativity" or "negative influences."

You will need: a shot of strong alcohol, a new, unsealed Witch Bottle, dragon's blood oil, and purifying incense such as cedar or sage.

⊚ *Have the hexee stand in the center of the room. Cast a circle around the person and yourself, as you normally would.*

⊚ *Say:*

We come this day/night to clear [person's name] of negative influences.

Hex-Breaking

Look the hexee in the eye and ask:

Is it truly your wish to be cleared of negative energy from within and without, and any external negative influences?

If the person says yes, then you may continue.

◎ *Light the incense. (If the hexee has allergies or is bothered by smoke an oil diffuser will also work, though it is a bit cumbersome.) Waft the smoke towards the person's head, heart, abdomen, feet, and back, paying special attention to the base of the spine and the back of the neck. Say:*

With smoke and herbs I cleanse you.
The embrace of the earth absorbs all that is negative.
The power of [incense] cleanses away your burdens.
Cleansed and purified, your light may shine.

◎ *Anoint the person with the oil on the third eye, the hollow of the throat, the back of the neck, and the base of the spine. Say:*

With dragon's blood I strengthen you.
As this oil absorbs into your skin, so will the strength of a dragon.
Strength of body, strength of mind, strength of spirit.
Strength to fight all that would hold and control you against your true will.

◎

Pour the shot of alcohol and hold it in your dominant hand. Say:

With the burn of liquor we shall burn out negativity and any influences that do not belong.

⊚ *Hand the unsealed Witch Bottle to the hexee. Instruct the hexee to take the shot and swirl it in his or her mouth, but not to swallow. As the hexee holds the alcohol in his or her mouth, say:*

Fire of liquor, burn away that which does not belong.
Melt its hold on [hexee's name].

⊚ *Do a slow count to 10 and have the hexee spit the alcohol into the Witch Bottle. As he or she does so, say:*

As this liquor goes into this bottle, so does that which has troubled [hexee's name].

⊚ *Immediately seal the bottle and say:*

The negativity is now gone, trapped in this bottle of glass and pins. You will be troubled no more.

⊚ *Bury the bottle.*

- 12 -
In Case of Emergency, Break Glass

If all else has failed...

The following are some extraordinarily strong protective measures to be used only when all else fails and there is no one you can call on for help. In order to perform these measures effectively, you will need to be quite comfortable performing all of the protective measures mentioned previously. If performed incorrectly, these measures will not work and can backfire. Do not perform them unless you absolutely must.

When things go bump in the night and the previous methods have failed, then it is time to bump back. There are two significant dangers to this kind of magick:

1. As Nietzsche said: "If you stare into the abyss long enough the abyss stares into you." When working with shadow magick, there is always a danger of crossing the line into unethical behavior. That is why I say to use this ritual only when absolutely necessary. This ritual will not just cleanse; it will scour. It will leave things a blank slate. And if you're banishing an entity, it won't just make it go away. It will kill it.

2. These protective measures call on extremely potent (and none-too-kind) entities, and they are not to be trifled with. There is always a price for their aid. You may not reckon it for years, and you may not like it. Do not perform these measures unless you have no other option.

SHADOW PROTECTION

The following is an extremely potent form of shield that will hide the caster from negative entities and will actually grow stronger when attacked. The danger is that the shield can grow so strong that it is difficult to dispel, or could even develop a mind of its own.

⊚ *Begin by envisioning a disk of black shadows swirling just beneath your feet. Envision these shadows growing and flowing in a counterclockwise spiral until they completely encircle your body.*

⊚ *Take a deep breath in and envision yourself completely hidden within the shadows. Gather that intent into your breath. As you exhale, breathe your intent into the shadows, empowering them.*

In Case of Emergency, Break Glass

◎ *Take a deep breath in and envision the shadows absorbing all negativity directed at you. The shadows will absorb the negative energy and use it to strengthen themselves, growing thicker and darker. As they grow they will be able to absorb more and more. Gather that intent into your breath. As you exhale, breathe your intent into the shadows, giving them the ability to grow strong.*

◎ *Take a deep breath in. You are hidden and protected. Breathe out.*

When you are ready to dispel the shield, envision the shadows flowing down into the ground where they are neutralized.

Kali's Protection

This incantation calls on Kali, the demon-eating Goddess of Destruction from the Hindu pantheon. If you really, really need her, she will protect you. Say:

> *Kali ma protect me.*
> *Kali ma be with me.*
> *Kali ma keep me safe from harm.*

Repeat these words as necessary while you feel you are in danger. When you feel you are no longer in danger, say:

> *Kali ma I thank you for keeping me from harm.*

Scouring

This is an extremely potent ritual that will cleanse an area, banish anything that doesn't belong there, and set up strong permanent protections. This is not a ritual for beginners. This is not a ritual for someone merely comfortable with doing magick. This ritual is only to be performed by an adept, and then only when absolutely necessary.

This ritual is most potent if performed at the new moon.

You will need: a sterile lancet, alcohol for sterilizing your finger, a black candle, a white candle, a shot of very strong alcohol, dragon's blood incense, a quartz point, and a smudge stick.

◉ *Begin by thoroughly smudging the area where the ritual is to be performed.*

◉ *Take a few minutes to meditate on your purpose. You must know exactly what you intend to do. If you are removing an entity, you need to know what it is and what to call it. If you're cleansing an area of long-held negative energy it will help to know what caused it. You need to be absolutely committed to what you are about to do. If you have any doubts, don't do it.*

◉ *Cast a circle by using your arm, wand, or athame to trace its outer edges while saying:*

I cast thee circle of protection, to be a boundary between the worlds.
To create a place that is outside the mundane, where magick lives and breathes.
My ritual is begun.

◉ *Call the elements with the following evocations:*

I call thee great power of the north Power of the earth.
Power of grounding, strength, and foundation.
Come, lend me your aid this night.

I call thee great power of the east Power of air.
Power of intellect and wisdom.
Come, lend me your aid this night.

I call thee great power of the south Power of fire.
Power of strength, courage, and will.
Come, lend me your aid this night.

In Case of Emergency, Break Glass

I call thee great power of the west Power of water.
Power of healing, death, and rebirth.
Come, lend me your aid this night.

🌀 Light the dragon's blood incense. Let the smoke begin to curl in the air and then state your intent. The following is a sample; you should customize it to fit your situation as specifically as possible:

I come this night to scour my home. There are unwanted entities here and I will have them gone! I come to banish these goblins now and forever. I will not fear to live in my own home. My home will be a space of safety and comfort. As I do will so shall it be.

🌀 Begin the following evocation:

I call upon dark Hecate, goddess of crossroads, magick, and all the betweens.
Aid me this night. Give me the power of that which is beyond.

I call upon mighty Ares, god of war.
Aid me this night. Give me the strength and courage to slay my enemies.

I call upon fierce Kali, goddess of destruction and slayer of demons.
Aid me this night. Give me the power to prevail over all dark forces.

🌀 If you've performed the above evocation properly, you should feel the presence of the deities whom you've called.

🌀 Hold the black candle in your dominant hand and say:

As this candle burns, so shall all that are unwelcome here.
As this candle burns, all negativity here shall burn away.
As this candle burns, this place shall be scoured clean.

🌀 *Set the candle in the holder. Sterilize a finger with the alcohol. Take a deep breath and prick one of your fingers. Once you've gotten a decent drop of blood, wipe it on the candle, saying:*

By my blood I show my sincerity.
I offer this blood and my pain to you Hecate, Ares, and Kali.
Aid me and make this place clean.

🌀 *Light the black candle.*

🌀 *Prepare the shot of strong alcohol. You will be taking the shot in your mouth, holding it, and then spitting it across the lit flame. Make sure you aren't near anything flammable, and have a fire extinguisher nearby just in case.*

🌀 *Hold the shot in your dominant hand and say:*

With the fire of alcohol, the flame of banishing, and the will of the gods, I cleanse and consecrate this space.

🌀 *Take the shot in your mouth, hold it for a count of 10, then forcefully spit it across the candle flame. Say:*

By sacred fire this place is scoured clean.
By sacred fire it is consecrated and pure.

🌀 *Take the white candle in your dominant hand and say:*

As this candle burns, so shall this place be filled with purity.
As this candle burns, so shall this place be filled with light.
As this candle burns, so shall this place be sealed against any that would do me or mine harm.

In Case of Emergency, Break Glass

◎ *Set the candle in a holder and light it.*

◎ *Thank the deities you have called:*

> *I thank you dark Hecate for your aid this night.*
> *May your wisdom always be with me.*
>
> *I thank you mighty Ares for your aid this night.*
> *May your strength always be with me.*
>
> *I thank you fierce Kali for your aid this night.*
> *May your power always be with me.*

◎ *Dispell the elements by saying:*

> *Hail and farewell great power of the west.*
> *May I someday understand your mysteries.*
>
> *Hail and farewell great power of the south.*
> *May your fire be always within me.*
>
> *Hail and farewell great power of the east.*
> *May you always remain near.*
>
> *Hail and farewell great power of the north.*
> *May I always appreciate your bounty.*

◎ *Dispell the circle by tracing its outer edges in the opposite direction as before, while saying:*

> *I dispell you circle of protection.*
> *Return me to the mundane waking world.*
> *My ritual is ended.*

◎ *Ground and center.*

Having a hearty snack such as nuts or cheese, after the ritual can help your energy levels to return to normal.

Appendix

INDEX OF SYMPTOMS

The following is a list of some of the common symptoms of the presence of things that go bump in the night, with some of their possible causes. Please keep in mind that many of these symptoms also have normal, mundane causes that are far more likely to be the source of the problem than any metaphysical cause. Always look for mundane solutions before looking to magick.

Acting out of character and not knowing why: possession.
Anemia: classic vampire.
Apparition: intelligent ghost, living ghost, residual ghost.
Beautiful man/woman makes an offer that is too good to be true:
    Leanan-sidhe, sexual vampire.
Black dog with glowing red or yellow eyes: Hellhound.
Clothes torn without cause: boggart, pixy.
Desecrated corpses: ghoul, revenant.

Disembodied voices: intelligent ghost, living ghost, residual ghost.

Disappearances during full moon: shape-shifter.

Disturbed graves: ghoul.

Doors slamming: intelligent ghost, poltergeist.

Exhaustion after intense dreams: sexual vampire.

Extreme shift in personality: possession.

Failures of mechanical or electrical devices: gremlin.

Feeling drained after a good night's sleep: classic vampire, vampire witch, Nachtmare.

Feeling of being pulled to a particular spot: portal.

Feeling of being watched: pixy, goblin, intelligent ghost, imp, shadow people.

Feeling of dread: Djinn, intelligent ghost, goblin, imp, demon (severe).

Feeling of not being alone in one's mind: possession, doppelgänger.

Feeling of oppression: curse.

Feeling tired/drained when in the presence of a particular person: Taker.

Figures beckoning the living out into the night: hungry ghost.

Foul stench: demon.

Gardens withering despite care: boggart, goblin, phooka.

Getting lost in familiar locations: pixy.

Having hair pulled: pixy, boggart.

Hearing a voice no one else can hear: doppelgänger.

Hearing the baying of an enormous dog: Hellhound.

Household objects being mysteriously broken: boggart, goblin.

Ill health: curse.

Imbalance in nature: Elemental.

Irrepressible urges: possession.

Keening or screams heard immediately preceding a death in the family: Bean-sidhe.

Kitchen remains clean without much cleaning: brownie.

Appendix

Lack of Energy: curse.

Movement out of the corner of the eye: pixy, intelligent ghost, residual ghost.

Naughty children disappearing: Black Lady.

Nightmares: curse, Nachtmare, demon (severe).

Nocturnal disturbance of crops and livestock: phooka.

Noticeable lack of wildlife: goblin.

Objects moving of their own accord: boggart, intelligent ghost, poltergeist.

Out-of-place natural phenomena: Elemental.

People being found drained of life: hungry ghost, Leanan-sidhe.

Phantom smells: intelligent ghost, residual ghost.

Phantom sounds (such as knocking): intelligent ghost, residual ghost, poltergeist.

Presence of many metaphysical creatures that seem to originate from one spot: portal.

Prickling at the base of the spine or abdomen: imp.

Puncture wounds: classic vampire, vampire witch.

Recurring nightmares: classic vampire.

Sandstorms: Djinn.

Seeing a dark mass out of the corner of the eye: goblin, intelligent ghost, shadow people, doppelgänger.

Seeing or hearing a mass of spectral hunters: Wild Hunt.

Sensitivity to silver: classic vampire, shape-shifter.

Shambling corpse rising from the grave: revenant.

Small household chores mysteriously finished: brownie.

Small shiny objects being "misplaced": pixy.

Speaking in tongues: possession.

Time seeming to pass differently in a particular place: portal.

Tripping on nothing: pixy.

Uncommon bad luck: curse, demon (severe).

Unexplained balls of light low to the ground outdoors: Will-o'-the-Wisp.

Unexplained malignant mischief: goblin, demon (severe).

Unexplained scratches: intelligent ghost, goblin, poltergeist, demon (severe).

Wailing heard at night: hungry ghost, Bean-sidhe.

Wakening in the night to feeling a weight on the chest and not being able to move: Nachtmare.

Wasting illness: possession, nosferatu, sexual vampire, vampire witch.

Bibliography

"Baba Yaga." *www.oldrussia.net/baba.html* (accessed January–March 2010).

Barret, Francis. *The Magus.* 1801. Available at *www.sacred-texts.com/grim/magus/index.htm* (accessed January–March 2010).

Bird, Stephanie Rose. *Sticks, Stones, Roots & Bones.* Woodbury, Minn.: Llewellyn Publications, 2007.

"The Black Veil." *http://psychicvampire.org/blackveil.htm* (accessed January–March 2010).

"Boggart." *www.pantheon.org/articles/b/boggart.html,* 2007 (accessed January–March 2010).

"Boggarts." *www.magick7.com/ghosts/Boggarts.htm,* 2007 (accessed January–March 2010).

Borden, Adrienne, and Steve Coyote. "The Smudging Ceremony." *www.asunam.com/smudge_ceremony.html* (accessed January–March 2010).

"The Brownie." *www.sacred-texts.com/neu/celt/tfm/tfm130.htm,* 2007 (accessed January–March 2010).

"Brownies & Boggarts." *www.tqnyc.org/NYC063585/brown.htm*, 2007 (accessed January–March 2010).

"The Children of Lir." *www.ireland-information.com/articles/thechildrenoflir. htm* (accessed January–March 2010).

Colum, Padraic. *Great Myths of the World.* Mineola, N.Y.: Dover Publications, Inc., 2005.

Cuhulain, Kerr. *Full Contact Magick: A Book of Shadows for the Wiccan Warrior.* Woodbury, Minn.: Llewellyn Publications, 2002.

———. *Magickal Self-Defense: A Quantum Approach to Warding.* Woodbury, Minn.: Llewellyn Publications, 2008.

Cunningham, Scott. *The Complete Book of Incense, Oils & Brews.* St. Paul, Minn.: Llewellyn Publications, 2002.

———. *Encyclopedia of Crystal, Gem & Metal Magic.* St. Paul, Minn.: Llewellyn Publications, 2002.

———. *Encyclopedia of Magickal Herbs.* St. Paul, Minn.: Llewellyn Publications, 2003.

Culpepper, John. *Culpepper's Color Herbal.* Ed. by David Potterson. New York: Sterling Publishing Co., 2007.

Curran, Bob. *Dark Fairies.* Pompton Plains, N.J.: New Page Books, 2010.

———. *A Field Guide to Irish Fairies.* Vancouver, B.C.: Chronicle Books, 1998.

———. *Zombies: A Field Guide to the Walking Dead.* Franklin Lakes, N.J.: New Page Books, 2009.

Danelek, J. Allen. *The Case for Ghosts: An Objective Look at the Paranormal.* Woodbury, Minn.: Llewellyn Publications, 2006.

Denning, Hazel. *True Hauntings: Spirits With a Purpose.* St. Paul, Minn.: Llewellyn Publications, 2003.

Deren, Maya. *Divine Horsemen: The Living Gods of Haiti.* Kingston, N.Y.: McPhearson & Co., 1953.

"The Fool of the Fourth." *www.shee-eire.com/Magic&Mythology/Fairylore/ FoolFort/LGfoolforth/page1.htm* (accessed January–March 2010).

Froud, Brian. *Good Faeries, Bad Faeries.* New York: Simon & Schuster, 1998.

Bibliography

Froud, Brian, and Ari Berk. *Goblins!* New York: Harry N. Abrams, Inc., 2004.

Froud, Brian, and Alan Lee. *Faeries.* New York: Harry N. Abrams, Inc., 1978.

Gardner, Gerald. *Witchcraft Today.* Essex House, Thame, England: I-H-O Books, 1954.

"Get to Know Your Ghosts: Intelligent Haunt." *www.the-atlantic-paranormal- society.com/articles/general/ghostsintelligent.html*, 2007 (accessed January–March 2010).

"Get to Know Your Ghosts: The Residual Haunt." Jason Hawes. *www.the-atlantic-paranormal-society.com/articles/general/ghostsresidual.html*, 2007 (accessed January–March 2010).

"Goblins." *www.mysticfamiliar.com/library/goblins/l_goblins.htm* (accessed January–March 2010).

Goodwyn, Melba. *Ghost Worlds: A Guide to Poltergeists, Portals, Ecto-Mist & Spirit Behavior.* Woodbury, Minn.: Llewellyn Publications, 2007.

Gundarsson, Kveldulf Hagen. "The Folklore of the Wild Hunt and the Furious Host." *www.vinland.org/heathen/mt/wildhunt.html* (accessed January–March 2010).

Haggerty, Bridget. "Creepy Irish Creatures." *www.irishcultureandcustoms.com/ACalend/CreepyCreatures.html* (accessed January–March 2010).

Hall, Judy. *The Crystal Bible: A Definitive Guide to Crystals.* Cincinnati, Ohio: Walking Stick Press, 2003.

"Hauntings: Intelligent Spirits." *www.prairieghosts.com/conspirit.html*, 2007 (accessed January–March 2010).

"Hauntings: Residual Hauntings." *www.prairieghosts.com/resid.html*, 2007 (accessed January–March 2010).

"Hauntings Explained in Ghost Hunting." *www.ghost-trackers.org/hauntings_explained.htm*, 2007 (accessed January–March 2010).

Holland, Heidi. *African Magic.* Johannesburg, South Africa: Viking, 2001.

Holzer, Hans. *Ghosts: True Encounters With the World Beyond.* New York: Black Doge & Leventhal Publishers, 1997.

Illes, Judika. *The Element Encyclopedia of 5000 Spells.* London: Element, 2004.

———. *The Element Encyclopedia of Witchcraft.* London, Element, 2005.

———. *Emergency Magic! 150 Spells for Surviving the Worst-Case Scenario.* Gloucester, Mass.: Fair Winds Press, 2002.

———. *Encyclopedia of Spirits.* New York: Harper Collins, 2009.

Kingston, Karen. *Creating Sacred Space With Feng Shui.* New York: Broadway Books, 1997.

Klain-Hass, Michelle. "Smudging: How to do it—How not to do it." *www.sacred-texts.com/bos/bos054.htm* (accessed January–March 2010).

Konstantinos. *Vampires: The Occult Truth.* St. Paul, Minn.: Llewellyn Publications, 1996.

Lang, Andrew. "Anthropology and Hallucinations." *www.psychanalyse-paris. com/843-Anthropology-and.html,* 2009 (accessed January–March 2010).

"Legends and Boggarts." *www.jacknadin2.50megs.com/custom4.html,* 2007 (accessed January–March 2010).

Maberry, Jonathan. *Vampire Universe.* New York: Citadel Press, 2006.

Mack, Carol, and Dinah Mack. *A Field Guide to Demons, Fairies, Fallen Angels, and Other Subversive Spirits.* New York: Owl Books, 1998.

Matthews, Caitlin. *Psychic Shield: The Personal Handbook of Psychic Protection.* Berkeley, Calif.: Ulysses Press, 2005.

Matthews, John & Caitlin. *The Element Encyclopedia of Magical Creatures.* New York: Barnes & Noble Press, 2006.

McCoy, Edain. *A Witch's Guide to Faery Folk.* St. Paul, Minn.: Llewelyn Publications, 1999.

Melton, J. Gordon. *The Vampire Book: The Encyclopedia of the Undead, 2nd Ed.* Canton, Mich.: Visible Ink Press, 1999.

Miller, Jason. *Protection & Reversal Magick: A Witch's Defense Manual.* Franklin Lakes, N.J.: New Page Books, 2006.

Morrison, Dorothy. *Utterly Wicked: Curses, Hexes & Other Unsavory Notions.* St. Louis, Mo.: Willow Tree Press, 2007.

"The Official Shadow People Archives." *www.shadowpeople.org* (accessed January–March 2010).

Bibliography

"Other Creatures." *http://infinitysrising.tripod.com/id7.html* (accessed January–March 2010).

Owusu, Heike. *Voodoo Rituals: A User's Guide.* New York: Sterling Publishing Co., Inc., 2000.

"Poltergeist Activity." *www.prairieghosts.com/polter.html*, 2007 (accessed January–March 2010).

Rogers, Liam. "The Wild Hunt." *http://whitedragon.org.uk/articles/hunt.htm* (accessed January–March 2010).

Rule, Leslie. *Ghosts Among Us.* Kansas City, Mo.: Andrew McMeel Publishing, 2004.

Sargent, Denny. *Clean Sweep.* San Francisco: Weiser Books, 2007.

"Smudging." *www.crystalinks.com/smudging.html* (accessed January–March 2010).

Sucking, Nigel. "Witch Bottles." *www.unicorngarden.com/grimoire04.htm*, 2009 (accessed January–March 2010).

"What is a Residual Haunting." *http://theshadowlands.net/ghost/residual.htm*, 2007 (accessed January–March 2010).

Xenophontovna Kalamatiano de Blumenthal, Verra. *Folk Tales From Russia.* 1903. Available at *www.sacred-texts.com/neu/ftr/chap06.htm* (accessed January–March 2010).

Yeats, W.B. *Irish Fairy and Folktales.* New York: Barnes & Noble Books, 1993.

Young, Ella. *Celtic Wonder-Tales.* New York: Dover Publications, Inc., 1910.

Zell-Ravenheart, Oberon. *Grimoire for the Apprentice Wizard.* Franklin Lakes, N.J.: New Page Books, 2004.

Zell-Ravenheart, Oberon, and Ash DeKirk. *A Wizard's Bestiary.* Franklin Lakes, N.J.: New Page Books, 2007.

Index

Index

N

O

M

P

Index

Index

U

unobtrusive protection ritual, 180

using an energy ball, 172

V

vampire witch,
  lore of, 99-100
  removal of, 101

vampire,
  classic, lore of, 87-89
  modern, lore of, 90-93

psychic, 92-93

sexual, lore of, 95-96

vital statistics, key to, 20-21

W

watchdog charm, 175

water, 164-165

Wild Hunt,
  lore of, 48-49
  removal of, 49-50

Will-o'-the-Wisp,
  lore of, 51-52
  removal of, 52

Witch Bottle, 166

About the Author

Emily Carlin is a lifelong resident of Seattle, Washington. A magickal practitioner for more than a decade, she is the Grey School of Wizardry's Dean of Dark Arts, specializing in defensive magick and creatures of the night, teaching magickal protection to people of all ages and skill levels (*www.greyschool.com*). She is happiest when head-deep in piles of obscure and arcane books. Emily also holds a Bachelor of Arts degree in philosophy from Wellesley College and a Juris Doctorate from Seattle University School of Law, and is a member of the Washington State Bar Association. The author can be contacted via her Website *www.e-carlin.com*.